"Ben Stevens is to be thanked for this herculean effort. This is arguably Edwards's most influential text among contemporary Christians, yet few have the patience and ability to wade through the original."

DR. DOUGLAS A. SWEENEY
Trinity Evangelical Divinity School

"It's not every day that a book about the meaning of everything is written. It's also not every day that you find a readable, understandable, and downright fun guide to such a momentous text. *Why God Created the World* by Ben Stevens is just such a book. It's brainy but eminently accessible, and the prose crackles with electric interest and arresting analogies. I know it will help many hungry Christians to dig into the meat of Edwards's original text, which is quite simply one of the most important books ever written."

DR. OWEN STRACHAN
Assistant professor of Christian theology and church history, Boyce College

"The moment 'why' passes our lips, we are doing theology. With the mind of a scholar and the heart of a pastor, Ben Stevens directs the voice of Jonathan Edwards to this all-important question. Substantive and clear, this book provides concepts with which to articulate an intelligent answer."

CHRIS CASTALDO
Director of the ministry of gospel renewal, Billy Graham Center at Wheaton College; author of *Holy Ground: Walking with Jesus as a Former Catholic*

D0206772

Why God Created the World

A JONATHAN EDWARDS ADAPTATION

BEN STEVENS

NAVPRESS

A NavPress resource published in alliance
with Tyndale House Publishers, Inc.

NAVPRESS⊘.

NavPress is the publishing ministry of The Navigators, an international Christian organization and leader in personal spiritual development. NavPress is committed to helping people grow spiritually and enjoy lives of meaning and hope through personal and group resources that are biblically rooted, culturally relevant, and highly practical.

For more information, visit www.NavPress.com.

© 2014 by Benjamin Stevens

A NAVPRESS resource published in alliance with Tyndale House Publishers, Inc.

ISBN 978-1-61291-586-9

Design by Gearbox and Dean H. Renninger

Published in association with the literary agency of Wolgemuth and Associates, Inc.

Some of the anecdotal illustrations in this book are true to life and are included with the permission of the persons involved. All other illustrations are composites of real situations, and any resemblance to people living or dead is coincidental.

Scripture quotations are taken from *The Holy Bible*, English Standard Version® (ESV®), copyright © 2001 by Crossway, a publishing ministry of Good News Publishers. Used by permission. All rights reserved. Italics in Scripture quotations are the author's emphasis.

Cataloging-in-Publication Data is Available.

Printed in the United States of America

19	18	17	16	15	14
6	5	4	3	2	1

TABLE OF CONTENTS

ACKNOWLEDGMENTS

I have never understood the convention of thanking one's wife last, as I would have hardly been in a position to complete this book, or much else, without mine. Thank you for your support and patience, Becky. You are the love of my life. I also appreciate the support of my parents, as well as my good friends David Easler and Jeff Pudelek, who cheered me on from start to finish. Once the project was in its embryonic stages, I got invaluable advice on the content from two Edwards scholars, Doug Sweeney and Owen Strachan, and on the publishing process in general from two writers, Chris Castaldo and Matthew Lee Anderson. The project would never have seen the light of day without their early words of advice and encouragement, so a special thanks to you four. Austin Wilson was kind enough to look over an unsolicited proposal on a plane ride and then pass it on to Erik Wolgemuth, who worked harder shopping the proposal than I care to imagine. I'm lucky to be able to work with such professionals and am incredibly honored to have their representation. At several points late in the writing, I got great advice from friends Doug Becker, Cooper Blade, and

Benjamin Sutton. Finally, I have enjoyed working with Brian Thomasson and all the folks at NavPress. Thanks for seeing the potential interest in this content and for taking a risk on an unpublished author.

INTRODUCTION

For most of my life, I never thought to ask why God created the world. I had asked myself, "Why did God create me *specifically?*" which seemed like a more practical thing to wonder. But the answers I found to that question always struck me as shallow. I think that's because it's impossible to understand what part we play in a story if we have never grasped what the story is about in the first place.

When I did eventually get interested in the more fundamental question of why God created the world, I ran into problems. At first, I concluded that He created the world "out of love for us." But that answer is not very intellectually satisfying. We haven't always been here to love. At some point, we had to be thought up too. So what led Him to think anything up in the first place? There is nothing material in creation which He didn't already have beforehand, and the fellowship He had in the Trinity was better than anything we have to offer.

As I wrestled through these issues, I did so as someone who became a Christian early in life. I had enjoyed decades of Christian community and then studied theology at the graduate level. In some ways, I assumed I was the only kind of person who could find this kind of theological dilemma intriguing. So you might imagine my surprise at the way the question sparked intense discussions with non-Christian friends here in Berlin, where I live; a place which sociologist Peter Berger has called the "world capital of atheism."

For a while I found this phenomenon as difficult to explain as the question itself. But then it dawned on me that my non-Christian friends here like debating the question for the same reason I do: It's the prequel to the gospel story. You see, if the only possible explanation for God's motives in creating the world is egomania or loneliness, as some might assume, then that shows how incoherent the rest of the story must be. On the other hand, if the story does have a logical and beautiful purpose, that makes sense of the tension Christians see in our rejection of God's plan. Either way, it's the place where the coherence of the story rises or falls.

Look at it this way: The gospel is a solution to a problem. What exactly is that problem? The problem is a kind of deviation from God's design, a deviation from the reason why God created the world. So how are we to understand for ourselves, let alone explain to others, the tragedy of the Fall, or even the joy of redemption, if we fail to understand the genius of creation itself? How are we to make sense of the story, and the God behind it, if we don't know *why* He got behind it?

As far as I know, there has only ever been one book written on this subject by a Christian. It was a monumental treatise by the former president of Princeton University, the eighteenth-century theologian Jonathan Edwards, called *Dissertation Concerning the End for Which God Created the World* (1765, published posthumously). Edwards counts as one of America's most innovative thinkers, and for anyone with the patience and skill to wade through his book, he has a great answer. But his tone and grammatical acrobatics make the original text nearly impossible to read.

My sheer curiosity forced me to work through the book, and I couldn't believe what I found. In the midst of these complicated formulations, Edwards cast virtually everything in Scripture in a new light. It was the most arresting thing I had read in a long time, but I didn't think anyone I knew would be interested in laboring through the original. So the idea crossed my mind to turn my notes, which I had made just to understand the book myself, into a shorter work for non-academics. I explained the idea to the folks at NavPress, who knew a few things about paraphrasing because of their work on *The Message*, and we're excited about how this new version will set some of those ideas from the eighteenth century loose in the twenty-first century.

In his original remarks Edwards did not give a long explanation of his motives for writing. He simply dove headlong into this most important of all questions. I find a certain genius in that. I considered adding a bio of him at the front of this book for context, and in fact I have added a short one in an appendix. But I decided to follow his minimalist approach in introducing the topic for two reasons: (1) There are plenty of excellent biographies available about his life, and (2) I'm convinced the best thing I can do to interest you in him as a person is to do what he himself did—get out of the way of big ideas about God. Perhaps like you, I came to his book with little interest in him as a person, and my interest in his story developed *as a result* of his answer to my question.

I will spare you a lot of details on my strategy for reworking his original text, but as a general rule, the ideas and analogies are his, and the style and tone are mine. For serious fans of Edwards, I have added an appendix which explains my approach in greater depth and highlights the few cases in which I have updated or added an analogy to flesh out his point. Lastly, I have included his original first chapter in an appendix for A/B comparison so that you can get a feel for his style and tone as well.

The vision of God which Edwards communicates in this book makes it a masterpiece, and I think it ought to be read and cherished by anyone who calls himself a Christian. I offer it in this new edition in the hopes that it might kindle the love of God, and of His mind-boggling glory, in your heart as it has in mine.

PART I:
LOGIC

CHAPTER ONE

Motives: A Few Helpful Distinctions

Without a motivation rooted in His nature—not because of some circumstance or consequence of creation—nothing would have moved Him to take on the task of creation.

Why did God create the world? In this book we will handle that question from two angles. In part 1, we will look at what logic can tell us, and in part 2 we will look at what Scripture has to say. I know that many people will be worried by the idea of trying to determine things about God using logic and might find such a philosophical approach suspicious. So let me explain my strategy.

Disagreements come up when discussing an important question like this one, and most often those disagreements revolve around a logical inference. We read a text which seems clear, but because we don't understand the logic of the text, we conclude, "No, this interpretation can't be right." Reason alone can't help us decide why God created the world, but because that's where disagreements tend to start, I would rather tackle it first. This will be easier than backtracking once we are knee-deep in Scripture, and such logical work helps us see Scripture's straightforward answer in a new light anyway.

We need to begin by thinking logically about God's possible motives for creating the world, and motives can be hard to quantify. This chapter, therefore, will give us some vocabulary for the discussion. I want to explain the three most important layers of a person's motives: (1) underlying intentions, (2) highest priorities, and (3) personal desires. I confess that this chapter will require more logical heavy lifting than most other chapters, but it's worth the work. By the end of this first chapter, we will have already learned things that change the way we think about why God created the world. Let's dive in.

Underlying Intentions

To understand people's underlying intentions, you have to consider their goals, their objectives. And in any goal, there are means and ends. I describe that difference by talking about *preliminary goals* vs. *pure goals*. A pure goal is an end, something you want for its own sake. Preliminary goals, on the other hand, are means, things you do just to get to a pure goal.

If you have ever been sick, you know all about this. Your pure goal will always be getting well, but in order to reach that pure goal, you inevitably set dozens of preliminary goals: make it to the doctor on time; get the right medicine; don't over-exert yourself. Each of these becomes your goal, but they aren't things you want for their own sake. You do them to get something else, your pure goal: restored health.

There are a few advanced ways this distinction can play out. Sometimes a task takes such a long time that there are other preliminary goals in front of a single preliminary goal, and you may spend a long time checking boxes, completing other preliminary goals, before you ever get to a pure goal. For example, a man may sell some of his belongings to buy start-up equipment for a new company. He may hire staff and employ an ad agency to help him get the word out about the product. But in all that he does in selling belongings, launching a company, and sending thank-you notes to initial customers, getting enough money to take care of his family may be the unseen but always-present pure goal.

On the other hand, sometimes there are no preliminary goals. If you're standing by the pool on a hot day and suddenly sense an urge to go swimming, jumping in could fulfill a pure goal. So you don't have to assume a long chain of activities.

Finally, sometimes the same goal can be preliminary in one sense and pure in another. If you're trying to win someone's respect, you might do so partly for its own sake. After all, it's nice to be respected. But if you think knowing that person would help you accomplish some other goal, it may be a means to an end—a preliminary goal—as well. So, sometimes a single goal can be pure in one sense and preliminary in another.

This distinction applies to God as well. God has lots of goals. Some are pure while others are preliminary. Confusing His pure goals with His preliminary goals would make it hard to know why He created the world, so in anything He does, we have to first stop to ask where His action falls on the spectrum between means and ends, whether it's a step toward a pure goal or the pure goal itself.

Highest Priorities

Highest priorities are a different lens through which to observe a person's goals. Let's say you determine that someone desires a thing for its own sake, making it a pure goal. That doesn't really tell you much about how important that goal is to the person *overall.* Jumping into a swimming pool and taking care of one's family may both be pure goals, but we should hope that one is a much higher overall priority in life. So we all have a hierarchy of priorities for our goals, from *highest goals* to *lesser goals*.

Sometimes a preliminary goal from one task can be higher than a pure goal from another task. Let's say a man inherits a huge mansion in his hometown and takes a trip back to sign the papers and close the deal. Several things run through his mind. He's excited about the estate, but not for its own sake. His apartment is already big enough. He's just looking forward to the prestige such a mansion will bring him. In this sense, inheriting the estate is a preliminary goal, but it's preliminary to a high life priority: prestige. On the other hand, he's excited about seeing all his old friends, as a pure goal. But seeing his friends isn't nearly as high of a life priority as prestige is, so he values the inheritance of this mansion—though preliminary to a pure goal—more than the pure, simple pleasure of seeing his friends. All that to say, occasionally a preliminary goal of one project will actually be more important than a pure goal of some other project.

Each of us has major life goals, and each of us has simple pleasures that sweeten daily life. To determine something as complex as why God created the world, we will have to keep our eyes on this distinction as well. Not all pure goals are lifetime objectives, and amidst the thousands of goals which God sets (and successfully accomplishes) in the course of human history, we have to distinguish between the lesser ones and the highest one.

Personal Desires

To complete our understanding of motives and goals, we need to add one important final layer: personality and experiences.

Goals don't get formulated in vacuums. They are developed by people with personal desires. So you should always consider whether a goal stems from something inherent in someone's personality (an absolute goal) or because of an experience that person had in the course of life (a consequential goal).

Take the example of a successful young man who comes from a big family and has plenty of good friends. He always has people to talk to, but he still longs to find a woman to marry. Does that desire come from some prolonged experience of loneliness or because of something inherent about who he is? In most cases we would say it's simply inherent. It's not a response to something. That makes it an absolute goal.

Let's say he finds a wife and they eventually start a family. Over time he may develop ideas of what it means to be a good father and outline an entire philosophy about raising children. It's important to remember, though, that he didn't fall in love with his wife *for his children's sake*. He fell in love with his wife due to an absolute goal. His children's existence and all his goals regarding them are simply consequences of his pursuit of a more inherent, absolute goal. This doesn't mean his children and his hopes for them are any less important. It just reminds us that they are consequential goals and so can't be the explanations for things which he did before they existed.

Conclusion

There are several immediate takeaways from all of these categories. Take this last set, for example. We are a consequence of God's decision to create. Now that we are here, He loves us. He even decided to enter human history to save us. But all of that comes as a consequence of His initial decision to create something at all. So what motivated that initial decision? What was His absolute goal?

We always start with ourselves. But if we aren't eternal, then something which is eternal, some absolute goal which was important to God before the idea of creation, must be what motivated Him to start the process. Think of it like this. Is it possible that God could have created the world out of pity for us? No. You can't pity something that doesn't exist. Pity assumes the existence of the one to be pitied. The same applies to love. It sounds poetic to say God created the world out of His love for us, but that assumes that we have always been here to love. We weren't. We had to be thought up. So why did God think us up in the first place?

God's love for justice and hatred of injustice explain why He does some things in human history now. They are, without a doubt, part of His consequential goals. But that should not lead us to think that He created the world in order to have the pleasure of settling our disputes. In fact, we have to suppose that something earlier—something more basic and inherent—must have motivated Him to create in the first place.

Without a motivation rooted in *His* nature—not because of some circumstance or consequence of creation—nothing would have moved Him to take on the task of creation. Therefore an original, absolute goal must have led to it. That inherent desire is the fountainhead of all creation and in fact of all other goals.

"So," you ask, "what *is* that absolute, pure goal?" To answer a question like that, we will simply have to take a closer look at God's personality.

DISCUSSION QUESTIONS

1. Edwards offers a number of distinctions in this chapter and says they will help us ask the right questions. How would you explain these distinctions in your own words?

2. What are some of your "absolute pure goals"?

3. Describe your feelings as you hear Edwards explain that neither pity nor love for us seems like it could be the reason that first motivated God to create the world.

4. Is the line of thinking that Edwards takes here something that's completely new to you, relatively familiar to you, or somewhere in between?

CHAPTER TWO

Good, True, and Beautiful: First Steps Toward an Answer

Creation must have arisen because of the way it accomplishes something God values.

Let's begin by considering the implications of what Christians already agree on about God's personality. That will greatly reduce the scope of the things we need to consider, and given the size of this topic, that reduction would be a relief. Christians from across the spectrum agree on a surprising number of things on this point, but let me list the two which I think help us zero in on an answer most quickly.

First, we agree that God is glorious and happy, independent of any external circumstances. His glory and happiness are eternal, and He doesn't live in fear that someone will steal or wound His joy. Secondly, we agree that the universe receives everything from God's hand and consequently has nothing to give back to Him which He didn't already have before creation.

These are not radical Christian convictions, but they go a long way toward eliminating many popular suggestions about why God created the world. I would summarize their implications like this: *If God does not need, and cannot receive, anything new from something He creates, then He must not have created in order to fill a need He had.*

With one stroke, this wipes out much of what the world's pagan religions have thought about their gods for millennia. But at the same time, it raises another question: If God didn't create because of a need He had, then what prompted Him to create at all? I think the most logical conclusion is that *if creation does not arise to fulfill some need that God has, then it must arise because of the way it accomplishes something that He values.*

This short set of considerations has already gotten us most of the way to our answer. Let's take a final step by thinking about what makes things valuable. I think that piece will complete the puzzle.

Value

As I explained in the last chapter, some things have value because of the way they serve a greater purpose. We might say they have a preliminary value. In this case, however, we are talking about things which are inherently valuable, things which God valued before there was any creation. Broadly speaking, we might say we're looking for things which are, in and of themselves, good, true, and beautiful.

With this point in mind, ask yourself the question: What existed before the creation of the world that was good, true, and beautiful? I believe you will see that everything which existed before the creation of the world, which was good, true, and beautiful . . . was God. If there is a God who created the universe as we know it, then that means there was also a time when everything we love, which inspires us, and which gives us goose bumps, was all simply an aspect of His personality.

Life as we experience it now doesn't force us to recognize this. A man can experience "love," for example, whether he believes in or acknowledges God at all. But this is a result of creation. It's a result of the fact that God has diffused Himself throughout human experience. There was a time before the creation of the world when the distinction would have been invalid, a time in which the thing we have come to know as "love" was literally embodied entirely in one (triune) being.

Creation must have arisen because of the way it accomplishes something God values. God values things like goodness, truth, and beauty. And yet those words are simply labels we have come up with to describe things which were, before creation, all Him. So I think we are logical to conclude that *if God could have created the universe to expand and increase Himself—and, implicitly, all the things which we have come to know in the abstract as goodness, truth, and beauty—then that best explains the logic behind His decision to create a universe in the first place.*

Perfect Priorities

At first this may all sound very odd, but I am simply suggesting that God makes the same connection that we make in the course of properly setting our values and priorities. For example, we value things like paintings. But we would never value a single painting more than the artist who painted it. In fact we value the artist more because he is the *source* of such great beauty. Setting his value higher actually acknowledges the value of any one of his individual paintings. And Christians would want to take the last logical step and affirm that God, who first had the idea to make artists, should have an even higher place in our priorities for the same reason: that He is the source of artists.

The idea I want to propose is that the logic which leads *us* to value God more than anything else . . . must also lead *God Himself* to value God more than anything else. He must, or at least ought to, come to the same conclusion about the importance and value of His role that we do: that He should have the greatest priority because His existence and work lead to the existence and work of all other good.

Let me take this a step further. We believe that God is good, not just because He's divine, but because He makes perfect judgments and because He faithfully evaluates and appraises whatever He sees. In contrast to the often haphazard way humans put one thing before another, God uses accurate weights and measures. So, although it seems strange at first, we put God's judgment into question if we assume that He doesn't accurately esteem the most valuable entity imaginable: Himself.

Beyond Piety

For some of you, this will sound pious but unreasonable, so let me close out the chapter by talking about value in slightly less religious language. How should things be appraised? Simply stated, I think we should appraise something by considering how good or beautiful it is, and how much of it we have. Something found everywhere which is nonetheless useless (think "dust") doesn't multiply out to value much, and something very, very beautiful which doesn't exist (think "the bus-sized diamond no one has") will also not be appraised very highly.

To determine what kind of a value to assign to God, then, one simply has to consider Him in light of the "goodness times availability" equation. When we do so, two things become apparent. First, as the source of all goodness, truth, and beauty, God ought to be seen as the most valuable entity imaginable. The total value of all created beings combined would by definition pale in comparison to their source. So the fact that He, secondly, cannot be exhausted and exists only to grow and grow, further deepening and increasing goodness, truth, and beauty, means we ought to look on Him as incomparably valuable. Logic demands that we appraise Him as high as possible.

Whether in His creating, preserving, using, changing, or destroying, we should have the highest reverence for God's actions and purposes. It further follows that we are logically, properly *subordinate* to Him. That's not a word we use very often, but in light of His role in reality, it seems rational to hope that He should have supreme discretion over history and to think that our value for God should be the compass which guides all our actions. So let me connect that to the point I made earlier.

We established that God didn't create because of a need but because it accomplishes something He values. And if He is wise, He would put forward as most valuable that which was the source of the greatest and most transcendent goodness, truth, and beauty. That is Himself. So God ought to act, in regard to all events in the universe, with an impossibly high regard for Himself. That would simultaneously be the most logical thing and the most loving thing for Him to do.

Conclusion

I recognize that in some ways, the thesis I have offered here raises as many questions as it answers. But we still have plenty of time to fill in the gaps and think through the implications. For now, I believe it is logical to conclude that:

1. God created not out of a need He had but because of the way creation accomplished something He valued.

2. God ought to value Himself and His attributes more than anything.

3. Creation must have resulted from the way God saw the value of expanding Himself: His goodness, truth, beauty, and all the things which are a part of Him.

That is my theory in its most essential form. What it means, whether it is true, and whether we can know it's true—that's where we're headed now.

DISCUSSION QUESTIONS

1. Edwards decided to talk about what seems logical (part 1) before he talks about what seems biblical (part 2) in the book. How do you feel about that approach?

2. Finish this sentence: "If God cannot receive anything new from His creation, then He . . ."

3. How would you explain Edwards's thesis about "why God created" in your own words?

4. This chapter offered some provocative suggestions about why God created the world. How would you describe your initial emotional response to hearing them?

CHAPTER THREE

Set Loose:
The Fruits of Creation

By creating the universe, then, God essentially made the well of His own creativity overflow.

Whatever happened as a result of creation was God's goal. That's because God always accomplishes what He sets out to do. So as I thought about ways to check our thesis, I decided we should spend some time considering just that: What actually happened as a result of the creation of the world? Specifically, what *good* resulted from God's decision to create? Four things came to mind, and I think taking a look at them will help you determine whether or not this thesis makes sense.

An Explosion of Sorts

The Bible doesn't tell us much about what "pre-creation" life was like for God. We know about the Trinity, and we know that He was the same then as He is today. But that leaves a lot unexplained, doesn't it? We do not know whether creation was a new kind of activity for God, or whether it gave Him a chance to flex muscles He had never flexed before. But what we can say is that, whether it was unique or not, creation gave God an opportunity to demonstrate His creative and conceptual genius.

Though He was entirely fulfilled without creation, it provided Him with an occasion to indulge Himself in an artistic explosion of sorts, and things like His power, wisdom, prudence, goodness, and truth got to be put on full display. By creating the universe, then, God essentially made the well of His own creativity overflow. That's exactly what we might expect to encounter given our findings in chapter 2: that God created the world to expand and multiply Himself.

New Knowledge

Many of the world's greatest philosophers have felt that, in some hard-to-explain way, existence is *greater* than non-existence. For example, the idea of having a good friend doesn't seem as great as actually having one. And a well-crafted plan which has actually been implemented seems greater than one which was never tried. Ideas are not valueless, but we love to see good things come to fruition. That has led to the intuition that somehow *existence is greater than non-existence.*

You don't have to buy into all the footnotes which might come along with that philosophy to think that it makes some sense out of God's decision to create. Any good plan which God has would be better executed than not. Any potential for creative exploration and innovation He possesses is something worth pursuing, something that ought to interest us.

Beyond that, we might also conclude that the more people to experience Him and know of His plans, the better. That is to say, it's better for a greater awareness, or a greater number of people, to be the audience for the things He thinks and does.

You don't have to believe there was an inferior state of affairs before humanity existed to believe that our creation was nonetheless a fitting development. Just as God is excellent, and His expression of Himself is excellent, so a knowledge of Him is excellent. Our existence grows out of the desire to give that excellence a greater audience, so this makes creation a gracious decision.

From Head to Heart

I have said that God ought to hold an infinitely high value for Himself, and I have presented the idea fairly theoretically. But if He truly does so, then this self-estimation must affect Him practically somehow. It must move from head to heart. For that reason I think we are logical to conclude that God's value for Himself makes Him love His nature, and that it even leads Him to *love seeing Himself loved*.

This sounds again like something which doesn't befit God, but on closer examination it's a phenomenon we encourage in every other arena of life. If you love something, then you hope others will come to see it and love it just like you. You want others to see the praiseworthiness of your spouse, your family, your favorite sports teams, or the cultural institutions you cherish. And you love hearing others praise those things because that means they are sharing in the goodness which you have discovered.

God loves seeing people share in the goodness He has discovered, but in His case—as in no other case—the goodness which He keeps discovering . . . is in Himself. All streams flow back to Him. Therefore it makes sense that He might create a world in which His own nature was both the starting point for and the destination of joy.

God Overflowing

The well of God's creativity runs eternally deep. There is, technically speaking, no bottom. He will never have a "last good idea." This differentiates Him from you and me, as our creativity depends on His inspiration and the diffusion of His nature in our experiences. For that reason, it would be praiseworthy and benevolent for Him to set Himself to the task of continually overflowing. It would be good to know that He was *striving* to expand and proliferate.

If it would be good for God to do something, then we have reason to think He is actually doing so. This is implied in the definition of a good God. So let me restate and refine the answer to the question "Why did God create the world?" by stating this: *A disposition in God, as an original property of His nature, to emanate His own infinite fullness, was what moved Him to create the world; and that that unfathomable emanation of His goodness and glory was His absolute, pure, highest goal.* His work eventually developed a facet which relates to human beings, but that came only after the initial impulse to create in the first place. Because of that, we may conclude that creation begins and ends with God's desire to magnify Himself and expand His goodness into all reaches of reality.

DISCUSSION QUESTIONS

1. Why does Edwards think examining what actually resulted from creation is a helpful way of understanding God's motives for creating the world?

2. The chapter explains four inherently good, inherently valuable results of the creation of the world. Can you explain one of them in your own words?

3. How would you complete this sentence: "If you love something, then you hope others will come to . . ." Can you think of examples from your life in which you have tried to excite others about something which excites you?

4. Has the idea of a disposition in God to overflow His goodness, truth, and beauty ever crossed your mind or seemed implied in something you have read in the Bible?

5. In talking about God, this chapter used several metaphors about inexhaustibility, such as "the well of God's creativity runs eternally deep." Have you ever had an experience that helped you appreciate God's inexhaustible creativity or goodness?

CHAPTER FOUR

One and the Same: How We Fit in the Plan

When you experience joy, you are most nearly approaching God's most natural state.

Creation is essentially the beginning of something external to God. So it may seem ironic that I have been suggesting *He* is the goal of creation. Wouldn't it make more sense, in light of this definition, to think He might be making *others* the goal? This question highlights a tension not only in my thesis, but in Christianity itself, and because our ideas about the relationship between God and creation have so much bearing on the question of why God created the world, I think it would be worthwhile to say a few things about that relationship.

Unlike pantheists, who say *God is everything*, Christians think God is strictly separate from the external world. He is not inside of the system He made. On the other hand, Christians do not believe, as deists do, that God never intervenes in creation. Our position differs from both groups. We believe God is completely separate from creation and yet intimately and directly involved in it nonetheless.

Few metaphors perfectly illustrate how this works, but several capture a bit of the mystery, and they go a long way toward explaining how something external to God is still intimately a part of His plan regarding Himself. It boggles the mind, for example, to catch sight of the highest leaf on a great redwood tree, several hundred feet up in the air, or the deepest roots, hidden a day's dig down in the ground, and realize that both serve the purposes of the trunk. You often forget their connectedness when you stand there gazing up or looking down. Yet the budding of leaves and extending of roots of a tree are all efforts which terminate in the tree itself. Their reaching out doesn't make them less a part of the tree's purposes but more. So the seeming diversity of the tree's parts and all of its extensions has one single, unified goal: the tree's own *further* self-extension.

In the same vein, you might think of rays of light and heat, leaving the sun and heading quickly toward the edge of the solar system, as somehow becoming detached from the actual business of the sun. But the whole business of the sun, if I can so personify it, *is* to diffuse. It exists to spread itself. So its expansion and diffusion throughout the solar system are in fact the fulfillment of the process happening at its core. Whether in the case of trees or the sun or God, it makes little sense to talk as if their expansion into new places has nothing to do with their own most central objectives. In each case, they expand and diffuse because expansion and diffusion are their express goals.

Seeing God Everywhere

Leaves and light may make a strong case for this idea as it regards trees and the sun, but in what specific ways does creation reveal God's purposes? Are there concrete examples which show that when God is promoting certain *things*, He is most truly promoting *Himself*? Three cases come to mind.

The first is divine knowledge. Every good thought humans have ever had is an echo of a thought God has already had in eternity. You might even say it is an echo of a thought which God has had *about Himself*. Your mind and surroundings are the fruits of His contemplation, so when you think, you are essentially participating in His thoughts about Himself. You can't understand yourself until you understand Him. And yet, as you learn about Him and the world He has created, this knowledge spreads out His nature in you, which completes His goal for creation.

A second example is divine joy. For humanity, joy is a special or occasional state, something which often differs from daily life. Yet when you experience joy, you are most nearly approaching God's most natural state. Joy is a kind of desirable unrest and excitement about how good things are, and in considering His nature, this happens to God all the time. When you interact with God and grasp His goodness—even amidst the suffering and brokenness of the present world—you experience joy. And in the process of indulging your joy and happiness in Him, you simultaneously increase His presence in you. This completes His goal for creation.

A third example is divine virtue, and here I mean that most foundational and basic element of virtue itself: love. As we look out on the rest of the universe, we see trillions of miles of beautiful creation that are impressive but impersonal. God has given humanity a unique capacity for love, and you might think that here again is proof that God is not thinking about Himself. But if humanity exercises this ability to love and to have relationship, where will it take them? Where will they find ultimate satisfaction in such a search? They will find it most perfectly in Him. So in giving you and me the ability to love, God is giving us capacities which, in the end, always lead us back to Him. And this completes His goal for creation.

One and the Same Goal

These examples explain how God relates to creation generally speaking, but they leave one major question lingering: What bright future is there for humanity if God's primary goal concerns Himself? That is, assuming the analogies are accurate, why should you and I think of them as good news? Here again the thesis seems to create more problems than it solves, but I think one last example will tie these ideas together into a coherent whole. The example is that of a diamond.

What is it that we cherish about diamonds? We cherish the way they sparkle and reflect the light. That is, we value them because they magnify and reveal something else. Our admiration for the things themselves is a bit ironic. The beauty we see in a gemstone is really just the beauty of the light. What value would diamonds have in a dark world?

There is no dichotomy between a diamond's desire to sparkle and the sun's desire to shine. In fact, from the point of view of the diamond, these two goals are inseparable. When you rush to see a shiny new diamond on someone's finger, you are in fact, knowingly or unknowingly, rushing to admire how beautiful the light can be when seen through a vessel made specifically to reflect it well. And the diamond you find on that finger will be beautiful only *insofar* as the sun shines brightly.

We know that we are derivatives of God and that we need His grace for forgiveness. But I believe we often evade the truth that we need His grace for life and flourishing as well. His expansion into all reaches of reality is directly bound up with our search for love, joy, and profundity. These things are only found in Him, and they will only ever be found in us, and in our experience, to the extent that He Himself is in us and in our experience. As I believe diamonds illustrate, God's mission to increase Himself not only aids humanity's desire to flourish, it is mankind's only *hope* for it.

This goes a long way toward explaining Christ's mission as well. We are vessels that were originally made to reflect, and to be channels for, God's transcendently good light. But we have attempted to become our own light and have haphazardly "recut the diamond," altering and damaging the way it functions. Christ came perfectly reflecting God's light, died for our crime of recutting diamonds we didn't own, and made it possible for us to be recut and then refilled with God's light.

Conclusion

It is no contradiction that God magnifies Himself and that we simultaneously flourish. I believe God looks at these two goals as one and the same. Just as a father looks at the well-being of his family as one and the same with his own, seeing all of their destinies as interwoven, so I believe God looks at the well-being of those who love Him and are called according to His purpose. We are the pinnacle of His self-expansion, and because we will grow in our conformity to Him more and more over the course of eternity, His self-identification with our well-being only makes sense. *All in all, I believe it is incredibly good news for humanity that God created the world with the primary goal of expanding Himself into all reaches of reality.*

DISCUSSION QUESTIONS

1. What are two views about God's relationship to creation that conflict with Christianity's view, and how do they differ from it?

2. Edwards uses trees and the sun as examples from nature that illustrate the way expansion can be intimately woven into a central goal. Can you think of any other examples that illustrate the same thing?

3. How does your capacity to love hint that God created the world to expand Himself and be known?

4. Many people think that mankind will be doomed to eternal boredom if God's main goal is expanding Himself. How would you argue that this critique poses a false dichotomy?

5. Edwards says that God's goal to glorify Himself is one and the same with our goal of flourishing and finding joy. Can you think of any moments in your life as a Christian when the intersection of these two desires (God's desire and your own) was made inescapably clear to you?

CHAPTER FIVE

Objections: Examining God's Character

We live in a world in which mankind sees itself, not God,
at the center of the plan.

As I considered the content of the past few chapters, four major critiques came to mind which I might logically raise against the thesis myself. We have handled some of them in passing, but so that we don't move along without giving these allegations a chance to be heard, let me state them as strongly as I can and then try to respond. Hopefully this will round off the logical case I have been trying to make and help you decide whether this thesis is the best commonsense answer to our question.

Objection: God Is Fully Glorified Already

It is absurd to say God created the world to glorify Himself or to obtain some new glory. He has been fully glorified in the Trinity from all eternity. Why would someone inherently infinite need to expand? That is, how could God possibly be added to, or be made happier, or be further advanced, if He already possesses all of these things to the maximal extent?

First, this understandable critique grows out of a misunderstanding about the way God's happiness works. It's true that God is absolutely self-sufficient and infinite, but that does not mean He never takes pleasure in anything He does now. God's nature does not condemn Him to a static state in which He may not get excited about a new project for fear it might make Him look incomplete. Furthermore, the joy He has in the outcome of creation does not mean He is dependent on it. Is the sun dependent on, or unfulfilled without, a diamond that reflects it?

Second, the objection suggests that God's infinite nature would incline Him not to take on new projects. But don't we all agree that God *has* taken on a new project in creation? And can you think of any scenario in which creation wasn't to fulfill some desire God had? Our existence and the fact that God sought to fulfill *some* goal by creating the world make a strong case that God still has desires, His infinite nature notwithstanding. So I believe we have reason to question the logic of the objection.

Finally, some people may think that my thesis about God's goals weakens His independence—that it means He depends on creation in order to become fully self-actualized. This critique seems much less plausible when you consider the implications of the alternative option, that God made the world for humanity's sake. Would making His success dependent on our approval of the project lead to greater independence for Him? I don't see how. Assuming that God did decide to create the world (an assumption I think we all have), I believe the thesis I have presented best explains how God could have created while remaining self-sufficient and independent from it at the same time.

This first objection begins logically, and it has a great deal of rhetorical force. But in calling every new action a deficiency in God's nature, it inadvertently hems Him in from doing anything He enjoys. And in suggesting that He would be more independent if He had to depend on us for success, it leads to the very kind of understanding of God which it set out to avoid.

Objection: God Is Not an Egomaniac

It is selfish to make your private interests the governing principle for every decision in life, and any such inclination or narrowness stems from a fallen nature. Why would we ascribe such a narrow, sin-colored set of priorities to a perfect, sinless God? The thesis that "God created the world to expand Himself" results from men projecting their own egomania onto their Creator. Shouldn't we assume that God had a more charitable goal in mind than we would?

Why do we discourage selfishness? It's not because we think a person should have no concern at all about his own well-being. No, we discourage selfish views of life, in which a person sees himself at the center of the universe, because such views do not correspond to reality and because delusions to the contrary lead to destructive behavior. Why, on the other hand, do we praise selflessness? Not because we devalue the individual, but because we know selflessness better reflects an accurate assessment of one's importance in the universe. *Both the thing we discourage (selfishness) and the thing we praise (selflessness) are rooted in one's ability to accurately perceive reality.*

Consider God's own perception of reality, then. What would be the most accurate way for Him to perceive His role in the universe? Figuratively speaking, God is the center. So, though it seems counterintuitive, the thing we praise about selflessness in humans is actually present in God's high estimation of Himself: an accurate view of reality. God is not delusional, as humans would have to be, when He looks on Himself as the Fountainhead and Sustainer of all reality. He *is* the Fountainhead and Sustainer of all reality. As soon as you drill down to the underlying concern we have about human selfishness, it becomes apparent that God's behavior in no way demonstrates it.

Here's another angle from which to consider God's alleged selfishness. In human society, there is almost always a tension between one person's interests and another's. If a man pursues his own dreams and starts a great new company, this could inadvertently lead to job cuts at a competing company and therefore complicate another man's pursuit of his dreams. This may not be evil, but it illustrates how competing interests characterize fallen human society.

Keeping that in mind, ask yourself: Is there a dichotomy between God's interests and humanity's interests? Should our relationship with Him be characterized by a kind of give and take? I don't think so, and I honestly don't know how it could be. What could God take from humanity? And if He was to somehow give or forgo one of His rights to sustain the universe, would it not be humanity that would perish immediately? In a sense for which there is no parallel in human society, our interests are bound up with God's interests, and we survive and flourish only to the extent that His interests succeed.

Lastly, to anyone who still objects that God's motives are selfish, I would ask: Is not your very existence a fruit of His attempt to expand Himself? And if your existence itself is a result of this process, then what grounds do you have to complain that God's behavior *only* works to your disadvantage?

Objection: God Is Above Attention-Getting

It would be beneath God to run around trying to convince people—or create people—simply to admire Him. Whether He is worthy to be praised and whether we ought to do so, it would have been petty for Him to have created the world just to garner such attention from beings infinitely lower than Him. We might expect this kind of obsessive self-focus from dictators, but we should not think of God like a dictator.

Let me start again with the fact of creation—that for whatever reason, God *did* decide to create. The objection above implies that it would be petty for God to have put His nature and its fruits at the center of His plan. I can appreciate the desire to shield God from the accusation of being petty. Yet I wonder what in all of reality one might substitute for Him which would be a more worthy object? That is, if *knowing God* is too petty of an aim for God to have set for creation, what would be less petty? Where would He go to find something of greater substance?

We object to excessive idolizing and worship of human leaders, but not because praise is inherently wrong or because there is nothing transcendently praiseworthy in the universe. No, we object to the worship of human leaders because those people are not themselves the *seat* of all that transcendent goodness and therefore have no right to take responsibility for it, or to claim that they can produce such goodness on demand. Precisely that makes God different. God *is* the seat of all goodness, and He can produce it on demand.

To refute this third objection, you only have to look around. We live in a world in which mankind sees itself, not God, at the center of the plan. Has that made the world less petty? That is, is the life we experience, and this model of society, God's grand and glorious plan for us? I hope not. In fact, I think, as Scripture suggests, that this present life has been corrupted by a man-centeredness of which we will be relieved in the times ahead by a reorienting of all reality to its natural Godward focus.

Objection: God's Goodness Isn't Just a By-Product

We have classically thought that God was good to us out of the affection in His heart for us. Now we are being told that everything we perceive as His goodness is a necessary by-product of a default, mechanistic process by which He expands Himself. If God is "doing good" because He has to, or because that's what happens in the course of things, then that means He isn't good or loving in the sense that we usually think of Him. For God to be good in the truest sense, His love has to be free, unforced, and personal.

In one sense this is a false dichotomy, and we need not think of God's pursuits and ours as separate endeavors. They work out to mean good for us both. At the same time, the objection does correctly note that God's aims come first in His mind, and that they first came independent from consideration of us. So an analogy might help explain why this isn't the problem which it seems to be.

When your favorite sports team scores a goal or wins a game, you probably celebrate. And the shouting and high-fiving you do isn't meant simply as a remembrance of their victory but as a participation in it. It's an attempt to get the fact and experience of their victory into your heart. Question: Does it matter that the player who scored the winning goal was not thinking particularly about you, at that moment, when he won the game? Would you celebrate less if you knew he didn't set out to score that goal only and exclusively for you? No, and in fact your joy comes from the privilege of being a part of something larger than yourself (the team and its accomplishments) for which you have no actual right.

This is precisely what you and I experience when worshipping God. Worship is the attempt to get the fact and the experience of God's profound self-expansion into our hearts. We don't simply sing and read stories about Him to *remember* Him but to *be a part of* what He is doing, and as we soak it in, we experience the same thing those fans do: the privilege of participation in something larger than ourselves. This feeling of being caught up in something greater than ourselves is a sensation which would not be possible if God did not have any pursuits greater than you, and as in the case of our love for sports, this set of ordered priorities in no way detracts from joy or its effects.

Conclusion

For five chapters now, we have been talking about one of the loftiest topics there is, and the language I have used has often only groped for ways to describe it. Divine revelation will always be the better guide, so that is where we will be going now. I do feel, however, that this first discussion will bear fruit in part 2. More than anything, I think it has prepared us to receive the things the Bible has to say, in their most natural, unforced reading, as both logically coherent and as very, very good news.

DISCUSSION QUESTIONS

1. Edwards lists four objections that he anticipated. Did any of them match your own concerns?

2. Was there a major objection you have that he didn't address explicitly?

3. Finish this sentence: "As soon as you drill down to the underlying concern we have about human selfishness, it becomes apparent that God's behavior . . ."

4. Can you think of times when any of these objections have proved a stumbling block to you in your own worship of God? Have you ever heard others use them as the reason they could not be Christians?

5. Edwards says it would be impossible for there to be "give and take" in the divine-human relationship. What does he mean by that, and why does he think so?

6. Having heard Edwards's full answer from logic, has this idea begun to shape the way you read your Bible in any way? Do you think it should affect our prayers or the way we speak about God in church?

PART II:
SCRIPTURE

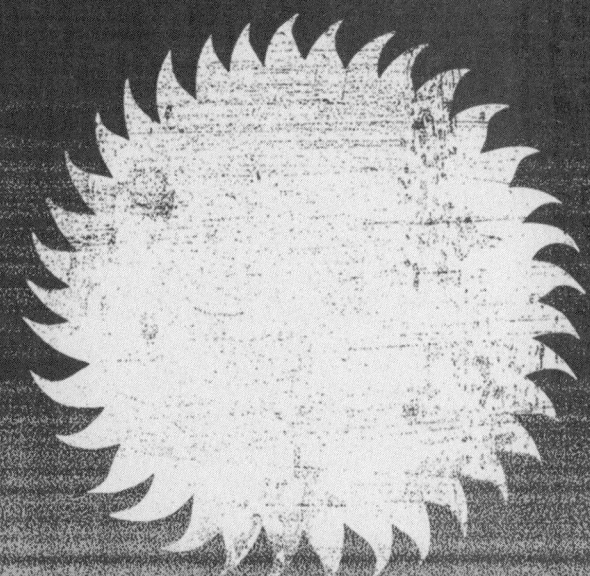

To and Through and For: The Clear Answer in Scripture

For from him and through him and to him are all things.
To him be glory forever. Amen.

ROMANS 11:3

From the first page to the last page, Scripture says God put Himself at the center of His plan in creation. It says He is both the source of its being and the purpose for which it was designed. A few well-known passages make this point:

> Thus says the LORD, the King of Israel
>   and his Redeemer, the LORD of hosts:
> "I am the first and I am the last;
>   besides me there is no god." (Isaiah 44:6)

> "I am the Alpha and the Omega," says the Lord
> God, "who is and who was and who is to come,
> the Almighty." (Revelation 1:8)

It is tempting to assume these passages just mean that God is somehow the oldest and that He will be here the longest. But it makes more sense to understand them as "I am the cause of creation and its goal, the fountain from which it flows and the ocean toward which it flows." That reading seems most natural in light of passages like:

> For *from* him and *through* him and *to* him are all things. To him be glory forever. Amen. (Romans 11:36)

> For by him all things were created, in heaven and on earth, visible and invisible, whether thrones or dominions or rulers or authorities—all things were created *through him and for him.* (Colossians 1:16)

> For it was fitting that he, *for whom and by whom* all things exist . . . (Hebrews 2:10)

The proposition we assembled in part 1 is so big and consequential that you might doubt that you could have possibly missed it in so many years of reading the Bible. Furthermore, to the extent that it may be a new perspective for you, it may be hard to accept emotionally. You will only be able to embrace this view of God at a heart level when you feel confident that it is the undisputed position of Scripture. So I want to use part 2 to help make that move from hunch to fact. My goal is to help remove any doubts or suspicions you might have about having been misled, or momentarily convinced of an extreme, one-sided view, by showing that the Bible takes this position from all sides.

How are we going to do that? Well, we are going to need to look at the issue from many different angles to make sure we haven't read too much into any particular passage. That requires a lot of material, so let's talk for a moment about where to find it all.

Where to Look?

No book of the Bible was dedicated solely to explaining why God created the world, but if you were to search through the many different books and genres in its pages, how would you know when you had found something of relevance? Here are the questions which I think will help us find the answer we're looking for.

First, let's get the obvious out of the way: *Are there places where the Bible explicitly states why God created the world?* If so, we should take those statements at face value. Fortunately, there are several such passages, which we will handle in a moment.

Second, *does God seem to have a particular purpose in mind for the moral part of the world, specifically for humanity?* If so, then that purpose will help you understand why He created. Why? Because humanity is the pinnacle of creation, and His goal for that pinnacle is very likely one and the same as His goal for the whole system.

Third, *does the Bible ever explain what makes something "good" or what lies at the root of beauty or truth?* These are the things which we are to pursue in life, so the closer we can get to understanding what makes them worthy of being pursued in the first place, the closer we get to understanding the aim God was pursuing in creating the world.

Fourth, *does God ever explicitly ask His followers to have a certain view of life or to behave in any specific ways?* Those requests or instructions might clue us in to His goal. I might add to this a fifth and complementary question: *Does the Bible ever explain the desires and hopes of holy people, of those whom it holds up as examples?* If so, then their behavior probably points to God's intentions and hopes for creation, because holiness is rooted in solidarity with God's purposes.

Sixth, *does the Bible ever explain Jesus' own stated mission or the purpose for which God sent Him?* Since Jesus is the head of all humanity, the moral world, and especially the good part of it, we have strong reason to believe that His main goal was one and the same with God's goal in creation.

And lastly, *is anything most frequently described as the aim of God's providence in general, the pure goal of His daily operations?* If so, then that information would be extremely helpful in understanding why He created in the first place. God created the universe for some purpose, with it as a sort of tool, and we can best understand the purpose which the tool serves by watching how He uses it. Over the course of history, through His many individual decisions and acts, it becomes possible to discern a larger cumulative picture of His plan. And the closer you look at isolated cases of His involvement in history, the more easily you see how they fit together.

I think these questions will be able to generate more than enough dialogue with Scripture to help us understand God's motives. Here's how we will tackle the task. In the next chapter, we will briefly define an expression which gets thrown around a lot but is rarely defined: "God's glory." Finally, we will spend chapters 3 through 5 sweeping across the Bible, looking from different angles at why God created the world, and conclude in chapter 6 by thinking about the ways the ideas from parts 1 and 2 speak into our twenty-first century context.

DISCUSSION QUESTIONS

1. Edwards quotes several passages in this chapter. Have you ever made the connection between these passages and the issue of why God created the world?

2. Coming into part 2, were there certain sections of Scripture that you expected Edwards to mention?

3. Edwards says we should start by considering *how to read* the Bible in the first place when trying to explain why God created the world. Is this something you normally do, either consciously or subconsciously, when trying to understand the Bible's answer to a topic?

4. Edwards offers a series of questions that we could ask when trying to get to the bottom of this issue. Are there any questions he left out that you think might also be helpful in our research?

CHAPTER TWO

A Word and a Process: Defining the Word Glory

The sun shall be no more your light by day, nor for
brightness shall the moon give you light; but the LORD will
be your everlasting light, and your God will be your glory.

ISAIAH 60:19

In the last chapter, we listed a number of questions that need to be asked of Scripture. The word *glory* is going to figure largely into its answers to those questions, and though you probably will have heard this word before, it might be hard to explain exactly what it means nonetheless. In fact, my thesis about why God created the world has often been critiqued on this very point, that I use the word *glory* like an exclamation point without a sentence, a catchall term which I never define very carefully. That's no small critique, so let's take a moment to look at how the Bible itself defines the word *glory*, first the term on its own and then the fascinating process which is usually implied with it.

The Word Itself

When the English Bible uses the word *glory*, it's almost always to translate the Hebrew verb *kavad*, which means "to make something heavy or weighty," or its adjective form *kaved*, which means "heavy or weighty." There's also the noun *kavod*, which means "gravity, heaviness, greatness, or abundance." So what are we to make of that?

Well, obviously the word can be used to describe physical things and how they are heavy or dense, and the combination of abundance and density gets at that last idea, of gravity. The word can also have a more figurative meaning, in the sense that we might talk about "weighty matters" or "profound topics" or describe the "fullness" or "perfection" of something. Lastly, it can be used to talk about value, with great things being *kaved* and worthless things not. But to summarize, it's the true substance and source of anything heavy, profound, or great, that which makes a "weighty" thing actually "weighty."

Because the term is used in so many different contexts, you would need to grab a concordance to see all the places it turns up. Yet to understand the meaning which is most important for our discussion, I think the word in the real-life context of the expression "God glorifying Himself" should interest us most. Let's consider the word from that angle.

The Process of Glory

The easiest way to think about the word *kavad*, or *doxa* as the New Testament writers translated the word into Greek, is as a kind of communication. As many language theorists have shown, communication is a process: There's the thought we have internally, the physical work of producing the sounds with the mouth, the way another person understands our words, and finally the effect which the words have on them. All of that is communication, though it seems to have several different components. That's also the best way to think about God glorifying Himself.

One aspect of God's glory is that substance which makes up His nature—all of the good, true, and beautiful potential *in Him*, independent of us, which has existed eternally. You might think of this as His *fullness*. But then there's a second aspect, by which He broadcasts or emanates that thing which is internal. Speaking creation into existence, for example, was an explosive instance of this kind of broadcast. Third, there's the phenomenon by which we perceive the things He has broadcast and emanated, and come to understand His intentions, and even what He's like as a person. And last, there's the change which this communication and broadcast of God's deepest internal nature can have on us personally. *That entire process* is God's glory, or God glorifying Himself.

This isn't my personal theory of what glory means. It's how the Bible explains it. Because it's a process, I wanted to highlight the big picture first so that you could see how the different pieces fit together. But now that I have done that, let me briefly take you to the places in Scripture where I think this understanding of glory, and of the process of God glorifying Himself, is made clear.

Glory as Something Internal

The Bible rarely takes time to dissect the different stages of God's actions like this. It usually treats them as a whole. We'll have to read between the lines a bit to see the contour of these stages, but they're there nonetheless. I want to focus first on the things internal to God. Where do I get the idea that glory is something internal, a kind of fullness? We see it, first of all, in the way the idea is used to describe completely normal objects and events. For example, things that people loathe are often called "light" or "empty" (that is, the opposite of "heavy" or "full"):

> And the people spoke against God and against Moses, "Why have you brought us up out of Egypt to die in the wilderness? For there is no food and no water, and we loathe this worthless [literally: light] food." (Numbers 21:5)

> And they gave him seventy pieces of silver out of the house of Baal-berith with which Abimelech hired worthless [literally: empty] and reckless fellows, who followed him. (Judges 9:4)

On the other hand, things that are valuable and substantial are often called "heavy" or "full," literally "glorious." In this way, glory means the substance of what someone has and possesses:

> You must tell my father of all my honor [literally: glory] in Egypt, and of all that you have seen. (Genesis 45:13)

> And Haman recounted to them the splendor [literally: glory] of his riches. (Esther 5:11)

> He has stripped from me my *glory* and taken the crown from my head. (Job 19:9)

> Be not afraid when a man becomes rich,
>   when the *glory* of his house increases.
> For when he dies he will carry nothing away;
>   his *glory* will not go down after him. (Psalm 49:16-17)

Paul even sets up a direct contrast between these two ideas—lightness and heaviness—to explain why we should keep our hope fixed on God's deliverance and not on our present circumstances:

> So we do not lose heart. Though our outer self is wasting away, our inner self is being renewed day by day. For this *light* momentary affliction is preparing for us an eternal *weight of glory* beyond all comparison, as we look not to the things that are seen but to the things that are unseen. (2 Corinthians 4:16-18)

Interestingly, Satan used this language, too, to sweeten his offer to Jesus, trying to show just how much was on the table:

> Again, the devil took him to a very high mountain and showed him all the kingdoms of the world *and their glory*. (Matthew 4:8)

So given this understanding of the word, we should be able to appreciate the contrast made between God's glory and the glory of anything else. He has so much more to offer out of Himself than any other could, and that's one aspect of what makes Him so much more glorious. He's fuller, denser, and richer in nature. A number of passages make clear reference to this internal aspect of glory, as a description of all that He is made of and possesses. For example:

> And my God will supply every need of yours *according to his riches* in glory in Christ Jesus. (Philippians 4:19)

> The sun shall be no more
>   your light by day,
> nor for brightness shall the moon
>   give you light;

but the LORD *will be* your everlasting light,
and your God *will be* your glory. (Isaiah 60:19)

And the glory of the LORD went up from the cherub
to the threshold of the house, and *the house was
filled* with the cloud, and *the court was filled* with the
brightness of the glory of the LORD. (Ezekiel 10:4)

In the year that King Uzziah died I saw the Lord sitting
upon a throne, high and lifted up; and the train of his
robe *filled the temple.* Above him stood the seraphim.
Each had six wings: with two he covered his face, and
with two he covered his feet, and with two he flew. And
one called to another and said:

"Holy, holy, holy is the LORD of hosts;
the whole earth is full of his glory!" (Isaiah 6:1-3)

If God is to give generously to others, the prerequisite is that He
must possess those things in the first place. And the Bible says
He has an inexhaustible, internal storehouse of all that is good,
true, and beautiful. So when you think about what it means for
God to glorify Himself, you should think first about this idea
of an internal storehouse.

Glory as a Broadcast

Of course, God's glory isn't simply something internal. In fact,
we often relate most naturally to the second component of the
process, that by which He broadcasts, or streams, His internal
nature outward. This is also an idea associated with the word *glory*
in nonreligious ways. For example, in 1 Corinthians 15:41, Paul

says that the brightness of the sun and the moon, the way they shine outward, is their "glory."

And when we turn to passages that address God directly, we find the same idea. In these texts, the word *glory* relates to a transaction by which God gives something or radiates something outward:

> For when he *received* honor and glory *from* God the Father, and the voice was borne to him by the Majestic Glory, "This is my beloved Son, with whom I am well pleased." (2 Peter 1:17)

> The glory that you have *given* me I have *given* to them, that they may be one even as we are one. (John 17:22)

> And behold, the glory of the God of Israel was coming from the east. And the sound of his coming was like the sound of many waters, and the earth *shone* with his glory. (Ezekiel 43:2)

> And an angel of the Lord appeared to them, and the glory of the Lord *shone* around them, and they were filled with great fear. (Luke 2:9)

> And the city has no need of sun or moon to shine on it, for the glory of God *gives* it light, and its lamp is the Lamb. (Revelation 21:23)

Glory as Reception

So to review, I first showed that glory is something internal. It's the fullness at the center of God's being. Second, it's the broadcast by which all the fullness of God gets sent or given out to others. But these two processes start getting truly interesting when we hit the third step, reception. That is, they become truly moving when people realize what's happening and when they begin to get the message. In some cases, they even ask for God to initiate this process *so that* they can receive it. Exodus reports the most famous incident of this request:

> Moses said, "Please *show* me your glory." And he
> said, "I will make all my goodness pass before you
> and will *proclaim* before you my name 'The LORD.'"
> (Exodus 33:18-19)

But apart from such dramatic incidents, we find dozens of examples in which glory seems to mean the reception or recognition of what God is doing in people's hearts. Here are just a few of those:

> For God, who said, "Let light shine out of darkness,"
> *has shone in our hearts* to give the light of the knowledge
> of the glory of God in the face of Jesus Christ.
> (2 Corinthians 4:6)

> "And *I will set my glory* among the nations, and all the
> nations shall see my judgment that I have executed,
> and my hand that I have laid on them. The house
> of Israel *shall know* that I am the LORD their God."
> (Ezekiel 39:21-22)

> Arise, shine, for your light has come,
>   and the glory of the LORD has risen upon you.
> For behold, darkness shall cover the earth,
>   and thick darkness the peoples;
> but the LORD will arise upon you,
>   and *his glory will be seen upon you.* (Isaiah 60:1-2)

For I consider that the sufferings of this present time are not worth comparing with *the glory that is to be revealed to us*. (Romans 8:18)

Glory as Effect

Finally, once God's internal nature has been broadcast outward and we have comprehended it, it begins to change us from the inside out. Once our hearts have registered who He is and what He desires through the first three steps of the process, the experience inclines you and me to praise Him and rejoice for all the fullness He has to offer. Ironically, this very praise makes us like antennas, taking the message God has broadcast to us and using our praise to pass it on. And as He planned, it starts the process of glorifying Him all over again. Several great texts in Scripture talk about this last step by which we are transformed and moved to praise. In 2 Corinthians, for example, Paul says,

And we all, with unveiled face, beholding the glory of the Lord, *are being transformed* into the same image from one degree of glory to another. For this comes from the Lord who is the Spirit. (3:18)

Paul later adds,

It is all for your sake, so that as grace extends to more and more people it may *increase* thanksgiving, to the glory of God. (4:15)

The Old Testament also embraced this idea and talked about how God's broadcast reaches and changes us, leading us to worship Him:

> The one who offers thanksgiving as his sacrifice
> > *glorifies* me;
> > to one who orders his way rightly
> > I will show the salvation of God! (Psalm 50:23)

> Let the habitants of Sela sing for joy,
> > let them shout from the top of the mountains.
> Let them *give glory* to the LORD,
> > and *declare his praise* in the coastlands.
> > > (Isaiah 42:11-12)

Finally, we hear of truly ultimate transformation in the book of Revelation, when God's glory begins to affect not just humans but a city itself:

> And he carried me away in the Spirit to a great, high mountain, and showed me the holy city Jerusalem coming down out of heaven from God, *having the glory of God*, its radiance like a most rare jewel, like a jasper, clear as crystal. (21:10-11)

Conclusion

At the beginning of this chapter, I noted how the Bible usually talks about these four stages as a whole, not by dissecting the concept as we have done. We spent most of our time looking at the steps individually so that we could take them in one at a time. But now that we know how to spot them in context, I think it would be fitting to close this chapter with a passage in which all four steps show up together. Take this example from Ephesians. Paul says,

> For this reason I bow my knees before the Father, from whom every family in heaven and on earth is named,

that according to the *riches of his glory* he may *grant
you* to be strengthened with power through his Spirit
in your inner being, so that Christ may dwell in your
hearts through faith—that you, being rooted and
grounded in love, may have strength *to comprehend*
with all the saints what is the breadth and length and
height and depth, and to know the love of Christ that
surpasses knowledge, that you may be *filled* with all
the fullness of God. (3:14-19)

Notice how each step plays a part. Paul says that his prayer will
be answered "according to [literally: out of] the riches of [God's]
glory." That's the first step. Secondly, he says he's praying that
God could "grant" us something. That covers the broadcast or
outward motion. Next, through that broadcast, he says we are
to "comprehend" the love of Christ, which passes all understanding. And finally, the goal is that we will be "filled with all
the fullness of God." *That* is what the Bible means when it talks
about God's glory and God glorifying Himself. Now that I have
explained what the word means and how it works, let's dive into
Scripture to see glory actually happening in history.

DISCUSSION QUESTIONS

1. When describing physical objects, both the Old Testament word
    kavad and the New Testament word *doxa* mean what?

2. This chapter said God's glory functions like another process.
    To which process did it compare glory and why?

3. Finish this sentence: "If God is to give generously to others,
    the prerequisite is that He must . . ." Can you remember

a time in your life when you were pleasantly surprised by all the ways that God had chosen to bless you out of His endless "storehouse"?

4. Edwards focuses on four different components, or stages, of the process of God glorifying Himself. Can you name those four stages? Were any of the four especially new to you?

5. Edwards concludes by talking about "glory as effect," the way God is made known by the effect that our experience of Him transforms us. Can you think of any ways in which God has been glorified by transformations in your life?

CHAPTER THREE

Glory: God's Work in History

All mine are yours, and yours are mine,
and I am glorified in them.

JOHN 17:10

A bit earlier, I outlined a set of seven questions which would be used to help find and understand Scripture's explanation of why God created the world. I think the easiest way forward would be to simply continue where we left off there and see what kinds of things turn up by posing those questions. I'll remind you of the questions as we go along.

First, are there places where the Bible explicitly states why God created the world?

God's words in Isaiah 48:11 imply that He made Himself the goal of creation, specifically by focusing on the expansion of His glory:

> For my own sake, for my own sake, I do it,
>> for how should my name be profaned?
>> *My glory I will not give to another.*

In other words, "if I refuse to give up on my goals and if I stay the course, the result is that I will be glorified. That would be the fruit of faithfulness to my own priorities." Here, God's "glory" and His "name" mean basically the same thing, as we will discuss more in the next chapter. And both the context and the text's emphatic tone ("for my own sake, for my own sake") make it clear that this is no preliminary goal.

In another case of very explicit reference to why God created the world, the apostle Paul says in Romans 11,

> Oh, the depth of the riches and wisdom and knowledge of God! How unsearchable are his judgments and how inscrutable his ways!
>
> "For who has known the mind of the Lord,
>   or who has been his counselor?"
> "Or who has given a gift to him
>   that he might be repaid?"
>
> *For from him and through him and to him are all things.*
> *To him be glory forever.* Amen. (verses 33-36)

In the lead-up to this passage, Paul summarizes God's plan in all of human history and explains the way God governs every event with the goal of glorifying Himself. He highlights the intricacy of this plan and the craft with which God wove so many seemingly irreconcilable subplots into one incredible, unified whole. But after considering God's justice, goodness, and sovereignty at such length for those eleven chapters, Paul finally breaks out of the logical discourse. And he says these words out of exasperation, to marvel at how profound God's design had been all along. "To him be glory forever" seems, therefore, to summarize the whole story.

Second, does God seem to have a particular purpose in mind for the moral part of the world, specifically for humanity?

The Bible says the people of God exist to see and experience His glory. No one makes this case more strongly than the prophet Isaiah:

> Your people shall all be righteous;
> they shall possess the land forever,
> the branch of my planting, the work of my hands,
> *that I might be glorified.* (Isaiah 60:21)

Two things come into view in passages like this one. The first relates to the people and their well-being. Here, God says they will always possess the land He wants to give them, so it speaks of a blessing that they receive. The second piece relates to God, that He will be glorified. Importantly, the context of these passages shows that glory is not simply a preliminary goal, or one which simply runs parallel to His goals for His people. In fact, it is the higher priority. When the saints partake in God's glory, it leads to their happiness. But it would be a mistake to think that God expands His glory first or primarily *for their happiness*. On the contrary, the happiness of God's people seems to be itself intended to play a part in the *greater project* of glorifying God.

In Isaiah chapter 43, for example, God talks of a future time when He will show His power and grace, deliver His people from their misery, and make them exceedingly happy. These things definitely serve humanity's interests and confer His blessing on them. At the end of all this explanation, though, comes a reminder of the greater goal:

> But now thus says the LORD,
> he who created you, O Jacob,
> he who formed you, O Israel:

"Fear not, for I have redeemed you;
>   I have called you by name, you are mine.
When you pass through the waters, I will be with you;
>   and through the rivers, they shall not overwhelm you;
when you walk through fire you shall not be burned,
>   and the flame shall not consume you. . . .
Because you are precious in my eyes,
>   and honored, and I love you,
I give men in return for you,
>   peoples in exchange for your life.
Fear not, for I am with you;
>   I will bring your offspring from the east,
>   and from the west I will gather you.
I will say to the north, Give up,
>   and to the south, Do not withhold;
bring my sons from afar
>   and my daughters from the end of the earth,
everyone who is called by my name,
>   *whom I created for my glory,*
>   *whom I formed and made.*" (verses 1-2,4-7)

We find the same in chapter 60. The whole passage focuses on promises about the future, overwhelming happiness of God's people:

The sun shall be no more
>   your light by day,
nor for brightness shall the moon
>   give you light;
but the Lord *will be* your everlasting light,
>   and your God *will be* your glory.
Your sun shall no more go down,
>   nor your moon withdraw itself;

for the LORD *will be* your everlasting light,
    and your days of mourning shall be ended.
        (verses 19-20)

God promises to rescue His people from their suffering and to glorify Himself. But while both are pure goals, the former goal seems to serve the latter. And this theme continues into the next chapter, in Isaiah 61, where God promises,

To those who mourn in Zion—
    to give them a beautiful headdress instead of ashes,
the oil of gladness instead of mourning,
    the garment of praise instead of a faint spirit;
that they may be called oaks of righteousness,
    the planting of the LORD, *that he may be glorified.*
        (verse 3)

We should be excited about what God's success means for our joy and for the liberation it brings from our self-inflicted bondage. At the same time, the Bible gives us reason to believe that even these things serve God's purposes of expanding Himself and His goodness. A few examples from other parts of Scripture will round out this point before we move on:

For as the loincloth clings to the waist of a man, so I *made* the whole house of Israel and the whole house of Judah cling to me, declares the LORD, that they might be for me a people, a name, a praise, and a glory, but they would not listen. (Jeremiah 13:11)

Paul articulates this concept later in the New Testament (see Titus 2:14), where he claims that God made His people to be a glory to Him. Their transformation from rebels to redeemed people demonstrates His effect on His surroundings, and what He stands for. The same idea is taught in Ephesians:

> In love he predestined us for adoption as sons through Jesus Christ, according to the purpose of his will, *to the praise of his glorious grace*, with which he has blessed us in the Beloved. (1:4-6)

This concept appears in a handful of shorter texts as well:

> Sing, O heavens, for the LORD has done it;
>   shout, O depths of the earth;
> break forth into singing, O mountains,
>   O forest, and every tree in it!
> For the LORD has redeemed Jacob,
>   and *will be glorified* in Israel. (Isaiah 44:23)

> And he said to me, "You are my servant,
>   Israel, *in whom I will be glorified*." (Isaiah 49:3)

> All mine are yours, and yours are mine, and I am *glorified* in them. (John 17:10)

> [He will come] on that day *to be glorified* in his saints, and to be marveled at among all who have believed. . . . To this end we always pray for you, that our God may make you worthy of his calling and may fulfill every resolve for good and every work of faith by his power, *so that the name of our Lord Jesus may be glorified in you*, and you in him, according to the grace of our God and the Lord Jesus Christ. (2 Thessalonians 1:10-12)

Third, does the Bible ever explain what makes something "good" or what lies at the root of beauty or truth?

Occasionally, and in each case it suggests that the virtue or value of any good thing lies in its connection to some way in which God is expanded and glorified. For example, Paul says in Philippians,

> It is my prayer that your love may abound more and more, with knowledge and all discernment, so that you may approve what is excellent, and so be pure and blameless for the day of Christ, filled with the fruit of righteousness that comes through Jesus Christ, *to the glory and praise of God.* (1:9-11)

This passage uses the term "fruit of righteousness." And what is desirable about this fruit? The fact that it brings "glory and praise" to God. John recorded words from Jesus which make the same point:

> By this my Father is *glorified*, that you bear much fruit and so prove to be my disciples. (John 15:8)

Jesus teaches that glorifying God should be the great goal of all our Christian pursuits. So having learned this lesson from Jesus, Peter suggests we should orient all of our meetings and Christian worship toward glorifying God as well:

> Whoever speaks, as one who speaks oracles of God; whoever serves, as one who serves by the strength that God supplies—*in order that in everything God may be glorified* through Jesus Christ. To him belong glory and dominion forever and ever. Amen. (1 Peter 4:11)

And if that is the intended result of our meetings, it should also be the aim we set for ourselves in our preaching. The book of

Revelation talks about conversion, repentance, and sanctification as *the same thing* as "glorifying God":

> And at that hour there was a great earthquake, and a tenth of the city fell. Seven thousand people were killed in the earthquake, and *the rest were terrified and gave glory to the God of heaven.* (Revelation 11:13)

> Then I saw another angel flying directly overhead, with an eternal gospel to proclaim to those who dwell on earth, to every nation and tribe and language and people. And he said with a loud voice, "*Fear God and give him glory,* because the hour of his judgment has come, and worship him who made heaven and earth, the sea and the springs of water." (Revelation 14:6-7)

Furthermore, just as we aim to be a part of God's self-expansion, the Bible says the best influence we could have on others is to live in a way that makes them want to experience His glory too:

> In the same way, let your light shine before others, *so that they may see your good works and give glory to your Father* who is in heaven. (Matthew 5:16)

> Keep your conduct among the Gentiles honorable, *so that when they speak against you as evildoers, they may see your good deeds and glorify God* on the day of visitation. (1 Peter 2:12)

This way of thinking is so ubiquitous throughout Scripture, and in the apostles' thinking, that they assumed their enemies would use it against them. In one passage in Romans, for example, Paul argued that God remained faithful and sovereign over His plan even when we rebelled, and that this provided a contrast which made it easier to see His glory. But because he understood his opponents so well, Paul anticipated their comeback, and when he cross-examined his own logic in the third person, he imagines how someone might argue against him:

> But if through my lie God's truth *abounds to his glory*, why am I still being condemned as a sinner? (Romans 3:7)

Paul dismisses this line of thinking as a slippery slope that makes evil good and totally distorts the order of things. But that he had to anticipate the critique and respond shows just how deeply God's glory was on the minds of Christians at the time.

Beyond these general cases, the Bible roots many specific behaviors and life decisions in the desire to glorify God. For example, speaking of Abraham's faith, Paul said,

> No unbelief made him waver concerning the promise of God, but he grew strong in his faith *as he gave glory to God.* (Romans 4:20)

And at the end of time, everyone will come to know and experience the truth that undergirded Abraham's trust, with the result that

> Every tongue [will] confess that Jesus Christ is Lord, *to the glory of God the Father.* (Philippians 2:11)

When people in Scripture are told to repent, it's always connected to God's mission to expand His nature:

> Then Joshua said to Achan, "My son, *give glory to the LORD* God of Israel and give praise to him. And tell me now what you have done; do not hide it from me." (Joshua 7:19)

The same can be said of the appeals and charges made to be generous and charitable while we follow Christ:

> And not only that, but he has been appointed by the churches to travel with us *as we carry out this act of grace that is being ministered by us, for the glory of the Lord himself* and to show our good will. (2 Corinthians 8:19)

What's the essence of thanksgiving? According to Jesus, it's the expansion of God's nature. After healing a number of people and seeing that only one came back to thank Him, He asked,

> Was no one found *to return and give praise to God* except this foreigner? (Luke 17:18)

This echoes the teaching in the Psalms:

> *The one who offers thanksgiving as his sacrifice glorifies me*; to one who orders his way rightly I will show the salvation of God! (Psalm 50:23)

Lastly, Paul suggests that we should respond to grace and redemption by thinking of ourselves as "not [our] own," but as part of something bigger that God is doing:

> Or do you not know that your body is a temple of the Holy Spirit within you, whom you have from God? You are not your own, for you were bought with a price. *So glorify God* in your body. (1 Corinthians 6:19-20)

I don't think Christians have grounds to look at God's glory as simply a by-product of their happiness or something which makes a nice accessory to the good, true, and beautiful. As we observed in part 1, so I think we can see here: Virtue itself is rooted in God's nature and a desire to see it spread and fill reality.

Fourth, does God ever explicitly ask His followers to have a certain view of life or to behave in any specific ways?

Several texts in Scripture tell us to look on God's glory, and our enjoyment of it, as the object of all our actions. A bit later in the letter to the Corinthians which we mentioned above, Paul says,

> So, whether you eat or drink, or whatever you do, *do all to the glory of God.* (1 Corinthians 10:31)

For that matter, when asked how to pray, Jesus taught His followers to *begin* by saying "Hallowed be your name," which means, "May your name be glorified" (as one can see from Leviticus 10:3, Ezekiel 28:22, and elsewhere). We will most naturally begin our prayers with the issues at the forefront of our minds, and because He put these words at the front of the prayer we are to pray, it's logical to conclude Christ had this desire at the forefront of His mind. As you and I try to follow His lead, we ought to have God's glory in the forefront of our minds as well.

Fifth, does the Bible ever explain the desires and hopes of holy people, of those whom it holds up as examples?

When saints and God-fearing people are depicted in Scripture, in their clearest frames of mind and most pleasing to God, they are depicted as focusing on God's nature and rooting their affections in His glory. The New Testament gives us many examples of this, not exclusively from one writer but from nearly all of them:

> *To the only wise God be glory* forevermore through Jesus Christ! Amen. (Romans 16:27)

> [Jesus] gave himself for our sins to deliver us from the present evil age, according to the will of our God and

Father, *to whom be the glory forever and ever.* Amen. (Galatians 1:4-5)

To him be glory in the church and in Christ Jesus throughout all generations, forever and ever. Amen. (Ephesians 3:21)

To our God and Father be glory forever and ever. Amen. (Philippians 4:20)

The Lord will rescue me from every evil deed and bring me safely into his heavenly kingdom. *To him be the glory forever and ever.* Amen. (2 Timothy 4:18)

[May God] equip you with everything good that you may do his will, working in us that which is pleasing in his sight, through Jesus Christ, *to whom be glory forever and ever.* Amen. (Hebrews 13:21)

But grow in the grace and knowledge of our Lord and Savior Jesus Christ. *To him be the glory both now and to the day of eternity.* Amen. (2 Peter 3:18)

[Now] to the only God, our Savior, through Jesus Christ our Lord, be glory, majesty, dominion, and authority, before all time and now and forever. Amen. (Jude 1:25)

[Grace to you] from Jesus Christ the faithful witness, the firstborn of the dead, and the ruler of kings on earth. To him who loves us and has freed us from our sins by his blood and made us a kingdom, priests to his God and Father, *to him be glory and dominion forever and ever.* Amen. (Revelation 1:5-6)

But this kind of thinking was not simply an invention of the New Testament writers. David, the greatest psalmist of all, also said,

> Ascribe to the LORD, O families of the peoples,
>   ascribe to the LORD glory and strength!
> *Ascribe to the LORD the glory due his name;*
>   bring an offering and come before him!
> Worship the LORD in the splendor of holiness.
>   (1 Chronicles 16:28-29)

The same kinds of expressions are also used in Psalms 29:1-2; 57:5; 72:18-19; 89:17-18; and 115:1, and they are applied to the whole people of God throughout the entire earth in Isaiah 42:10-12.

We also hear that the saints and angels in heaven express their deepest desires with such formulations in passages like Revelation 4:9,11; 5:11-14; and 7:12. The clearest glimpse of this heavenly dimension comes in two well-known passages, one from Isaiah's vision and the other from the visitation of the angels to the shepherds announcing Christ's birth:

> Above him stood the seraphim. Each had six wings:
> with two he covered his face, and with two he covered
> his feet, and with two he flew. And one called to
> another and said:
>
> > *"Holy, holy, holy is the LORD of hosts;*
> > the whole earth is full of his glory!"* (Isaiah 6:2-3)
>
> Glory to God in the highest,
>   and on earth peace among those with whom he is
>   pleased! (Luke 2:14)

Whether in heaven or on earth, those whom the Bible holds up as examples seek God's glory as their highest, pure goal. So when we hear the church say, "Not to us, O LORD, not to us, but to your name give glory" (Psalm 115:1), we should not see this as a means to an end but as the whole project.

Sixth, does the Bible ever explain Jesus' own stated mission or the purpose for which God sent Him?

Scripture says Jesus' highest aim was to glorify God:

> The one who speaks on his own authority seeks his own glory; but the one who *seeks the glory of him who sent him* is true, and in him there is no falsehood. (John 7:18)

As Christ heads toward Jerusalem a few days before His crucifixion, the thought of the violence and the suffering ahead seems to rattle Him. So how does He console Himself during this time? By thinking of how it will expand God's glory and make Him known. In the mental debate which occupies Jesus' mind in the lead-up to these horrible events, He relies on His highest priority for guidance, and that priority is to make God's aim His own. That's the goal which seems sweet to Him amidst the bitterness of the ordeal, and that's where His thinking and desires finally come to rest. His belief that this act will glorify God becomes His only source of comfort during that awful time:

> "Now is my soul troubled. And what shall I say? 'Father, save me from this hour'? *But for this purpose I have come to this hour. Father, glorify your name.*" Then a voice came from heaven: "I have glorified it, and I will glorify it again." (John 12:27-28)

If we doubted this view of Jesus' priorities, we could read the prayer He prayed with His disciples on the night He was betrayed, literally hours before the beginning of the ordeal. Here's how John remembered it:

> When Jesus had spoken these words, he lifted up his eyes to heaven, and said, "Father, the hour has come; *glorify your Son that the Son may glorify you.*" (John 17:1)

This was not simply a formality. As before so now, He began by praying for God's glory to be made manifest because that was the animating passion of His whole life. And insofar as that was the animating passion of the God-man, you can be confident that that is God's own animating passion too.

Or does God Himself state clearly the purpose for which He sent Jesus into the world?

Of the many acts of providence which the Bible records, none has a higher place than the incarnation, when God entered human history in the man Jesus Christ. And in the prayer Jesus prayed the night He was betrayed, which we have already mentioned, we hear Jesus explain not only *His* intentions, but also God's intentions with the mission as well:

> I glorified you on earth, *having accomplished the work that you gave me to do.* And now, Father, glorify me in your own presence with the glory that I had with you before the world existed. (John 17:4-5)

Likewise, John had recorded these words earlier:

> When he had gone out, Jesus said, "Now is the Son of Man glorified, and God is glorified in him. If God is glorified in him, God will also glorify him in himself, and glorify him at once." (John 13:31-32)

The angels confirmed God's intentions at the announcement of Jesus' birth in Luke 2:14, which we have already mentioned, and Paul expresses the same sentiment they did, in his letter to the Philippians:

> Though [Jesus] was in the form of God, [He] did not count equality with God a thing to be grasped, but emptied himself, by taking the form of a servant, being born in the likeness of men. And being found in human form, he humbled himself by becoming obedient to the point of death, even death on a cross. Therefore *God has highly exalted him* and bestowed on him the name that is above every name, so that at the name of Jesus every knee should bow, in heaven and on earth and under the earth, and every tongue confess that Jesus Christ is Lord, *to the glory of God the Father.* (Philippians 2:6-11)

In his famous opening words to the church in Ephesus, Paul dwells on God's intentions in sending Christ as well:

> Blessed be the God and Father of our Lord Jesus Christ, who has blessed us in Christ with every spiritual blessing in the heavenly places, even as he chose us in him before the foundation of the world, that we should be holy and blameless before him. In love he predestined us for adoption as sons through Jesus Christ, *according to the purpose of his will, to the praise of his glorious grace*, with which he has blessed us in the Beloved. (Ephesians 1:3-6)

Later in Ephesians, Paul summarizes God's overall intentions, and he says the plan had been carried out:

So that we who were the first to hope in Christ might
be *to the praise of his glory*. (1:12)

He argues the same point in his second letter to the Corinthians:

[I know] that he who raised the Lord Jesus will raise us
also with Jesus and bring us with you into his presence.
For it is all for your sake, so that as grace extends to
more and more people *it may increase thanksgiving,
to the glory of God*. (2 Corinthians 4:14-15)

Here Paul simply built on the long-standing Old Testament view
of God's purposes in redemption, as explained, for example, in
Psalm 79 and Isaiah 44:

Help us, O God of our salvation,
   for the glory of your name;
deliver us, and atone for our sins,
   for your name's sake! (Psalm 79:9)

Sing, O heavens, for the LORD has done it;
   shout, O depths of the earth;
break forth into singing, O mountains,
   O forest, and every tree in it!
*For the LORD has redeemed Jacob,
   and will be glorified in Israel*. (Isaiah 44:23)

In summary, the ultimate and highest goal of God's plan to
redeem humanity through Christ is that He might be further
known, further expanded, further "glorified."

**And seventh, is anything most frequently described as the
aim of God's providence in general, the pure goal of His daily
operations?**

Whenever the Bible explains God's motives in general

issues of providence, it attributes His decisions to His desire to be glorified. The psalmist looks at creation and sees this purpose:

> O LORD, our Lord,
>> how majestic is your name in all the earth!
> *You have set your glory above the heavens.* (Psalm 8:1)

Taking up the same topic, Psalm 104:31 says,

> May the glory of the LORD endure forever;
>> may the LORD *rejoice in his works.*

And these ideas are on the mind of the "seraphim" in Isaiah when they utter these famous words:

> Holy, holy, holy is the LORD of hosts;
> *the whole earth is full of his glory!* (6:3)

These passages cover the topic most broadly, but Scripture also goes on to say that God's other daily decisions are governed by His goal of expanding and glorifying Himself as well. Through the prophet Haggai, for example, He explains the goal of public worship:

> Go up to the hills and bring wood and build the house,
> *that I may take pleasure in it and that I may be glorified,*
> says the LORD. (Haggai 1:8)

He fulfills promises and gives rewards to make Himself known:

> For all the promises of God find their Yes in him. That is why it is through him that we utter our Amen to God *for his glory.* (2 Corinthians 1:20)

That's why He warns us against and punishes sin:

> Then the LORD said, "I have pardoned, according to your word. But truly, as I live, and as all the earth shall be filled with the glory of the LORD, *none of the men who have seen my glory and my signs* that I did in Egypt and in the wilderness, and yet have put me to the test these ten times and have not obeyed my voice, shall see the land that I swore to give to their fathers. And none of those who despised me shall see it." (Numbers 14:20-23)

> And I will harden the hearts of the Egyptians so that they shall go in after them, *and I will get glory over Pharaoh and all his host, his chariots, and his horsemen.* (Exodus 14:17)

> Thus says the Lord GOD:
>
> > "Behold, I am against you, O Sidon,
> >   *and I will manifest my glory in your midst.*
> > And they shall know that I am the LORD
> >   when I execute judgments in her
> >   and manifest my holiness in her. (Ezekiel 28:22)

> All the people of the land will bury them, and it will bring them renown *on the day that I show my glory,* declares the Lord GOD. (Ezekiel 39:13)

In fact, both punishment and mercy serve the greater end of glorifying God:

> What if God, desiring to show his wrath and to make known his power, has endured with much patience vessels of wrath prepared for destruction, *in order*

> *to make known the riches of his glory* for vessels of
> mercy, which he has prepared beforehand for glory.
> (Romans 9:22-23)

At the end of time, when God subdues all rebellion and brings all things back into the order for which they were designed, it will be for His glory's sake. In fact, the punishment meted out will be greatest because it means being *away* from God's glory:

> They will suffer the punishment of eternal destruction,
> *away from the presence of the Lord and from the glory of
> his might*, when he comes on that day to be glorified in
> his saints, and to be marveled at among all who have
> believed, because our testimony to you was believed.
> (2 Thessalonians 1:9-10)

Conclusion

We have looked at Scripture's teaching on many different fronts and asked it explicit questions about why God created the world. We also asked it more general questions like why God created mankind, what He requires of you and me, what lies at the root of goodness and in the hearts of the saints, what motivated Christ during His mission, and what seems to motivate God's decisions on matters big and small. In each case, we found lucid and powerful texts which pointed us to God's desire to expand and increase His nature, and to push His goodness, truth, and beauty into all reaches of reality. Before I move on to talk about how humanity fits into all this and what this means for you and me, let me take a minute to look at the issue from a few other angles to make sure we have understood the Bible's answer correctly.

DISCUSSION QUESTIONS

1. Toward the beginning of the chapter, Edwards recounts some
    of the most explicit passages in Scripture that say that God
    created us for "his glory" or to "be glorified." Was there one in
    particular that you thought made the point especially clearly?
    Did this chapter change the way you interpret any well-known
    passages?

2. Complete this sentence: "Just as we aim to be a part of God's
    self-expansion, the Bible says the best influence we could have
    on others is to live in a way that makes them want to . . ."

3. Edwards made the case that we can understand why God
    created the world by looking at the way holy people live. What
    is the logic behind that assumption? Are there people you know
    whose lives have brought home to you the merits of pursuing
    God and glorifying Him in all you do?

4. On the night He was betrayed, Jesus prayed these words as
    recorded in John 12:27: "Now my soul is troubled. And what
    shall I say? 'Father, save me from this hour'? But for this
    purpose I have come to this hour." What was the purpose to
    which He was referring, which He mentioned immediately
    following the end of this quote?

CHAPTER FOUR

Then You Will Know: Glory by Another Name

But you are a chosen race, a royal priesthood, a holy nation,
a people for his own possession, that you may proclaim
the excellencies of him who called you out of darkness
into his marvelous light.
1 PETER 2:9

In the last chapter, I asked Scripture a series of basic questions as to why God created the world. The answers I found relied heavily on the expression "God's glory," and you might get the impression that this is the only way the Bible talks about God's motives. But there are many different turns of phrase and mental images which are used to convey the same idea, and each serves as a slightly different lens through which to look at the topic. To round out and complement what I said in the last chapter, I want to mention three more expressions the Bible uses. They point to a number of additional and insightful passages which flesh out Scripture's answer to our question.

For His Name's Sake

The Bible very often explains God's actions by saying He does them "for His name's sake," which seems to mean virtually the same thing as "to glorify Himself." The expression is used, for example, to explain God's kindness to His children, the people of God:

> For the LORD will not forsake his people, *for his great name's sake*, because it has pleased the LORD to make you a people for himself. (1 Samuel 12:22)

> He restores my soul.
> He leads me in paths of righteousness
> *for his name's sake.* (Psalm 23:3)

> But you, O GOD my Lord,
>   deal on my behalf *for your name's sake*;
>   because your steadfast love is good, deliver me!
>   (Psalm 109:21)

Forgiveness of sin is repeatedly described as an act for His "name's sake":

> I am writing to you, little children,
>   *because your sins are forgiven for his name's sake.*
>   (1 John 2:12)

> *For your name's sake*, O LORD,
>   pardon my guilt, for it is great. (Psalm 25:11)

> Help us, O God of our salvation,
>   *for the glory of your name;*
> deliver us, and atone for our sins,
>   *for your name's sake!* (Psalm 79:9)

> Though our iniquities testify against us,
>   act, O LORD, *for your name's sake;*
> for our backslidings are many;
>   we have sinned against you. (Jeremiah 14:7)

This explains the way Scripture often talks about the Old Testament's most famous moments of redemption, like God's rescue of Israel from its enemies:

> And who is like your people Israel, the one nation on earth whom God went to redeem to be his people, *making himself a name* and doing for them great and awesome things by driving out before your people, whom you redeemed for yourself from Egypt, a nation and its gods? (2 Samuel 7:23)

> Yet he saved them *for his name's sake,*
>   that he might make known his mighty power.
>   (Psalm 106:8)

> [Where is he] who caused his glorious arm
>   to go at the right hand of Moses,
> who divided the waters before them
>   *to make for himself an everlasting name?* (Isaiah 63:12)

And Ezekiel adds these words from God:

> *But I acted for the sake of my name,* that it should not be profaned in the sight of the nations among whom they lived, in whose sight I made myself known to them in bringing them out of the land of Egypt. (Ezekiel 20:9)

God spoke the same way about the Babylonian captivity:

> *For my name's sake* I defer my anger,
>   *for the sake of my praise* I restrain it for you,
>   that I may not cut you off. . . .
> For my own sake, for my own sake, I do it,
>   for how should *my name* be profaned?
>   My glory I will not give to another. (Isaiah 48:9,11)

According to Ezekiel, God showed Israel mercy because

> *I had concern for my holy name*, which the house of
> Israel had profaned among the nations to which
> they came.
>
> Therefore say to the house of Israel, Thus says the
> Lord GOD: *It is not for your sake, O house of Israel,
> that I am about to act, but for the sake of my holy name,*
> which you have profaned among the nations to which
> you came. And I will vindicate the holiness *of my great
> name,* which has been profaned among the nations,
> and which you have profaned among them. And the
> nations will know that I am the LORD, declares the
> Lord GOD, when through you I vindicate my holiness
> before their eyes. (Ezekiel 36:21-23)

He continues later,

> Therefore thus says the Lord GOD: Now I will restore
> the fortunes of Jacob and have mercy on the whole
> house of Israel, and I will be jealous *for my holy name.*
> (Ezekiel 39:25)

And when Daniel prayed that God might forgive His people,
he asked that God do this *for His own sake*:

> O Lord, hear; O Lord, forgive. O Lord, pay attention
> and act. *Delay not, for your own sake,* O my God,
> because your city and your people *are called by your
> name.* (Daniel 9:19)

Why did God create a people for Himself? Why did He redeem
and purchase them at all? For His name's sake. The passage

mentioned above from 2 Samuel 7 makes this point, as do these two texts:

> For as the loincloth clings to the waist of a man, so I made the whole house of Israel and the whole house of Judah cling to me, declares the LORD, *that they might be for me a people, a name, a praise, and a glory,* but they would not listen. (Jeremiah 13:11)

> Simeon has related how God first visited the Gentiles, *to take from them a people for his name.* (Acts 15:14)

This is also why the saints live as they do. It's the virtue they see in the spiritual and religious life in the first place:

> We have received grace and apostleship [from God] to bring about the obedience of faith *for the sake of his name* among all the nations. (Romans 1:5)

> And everyone who has left houses or brothers or sisters or father or mother or children or lands, *for my name's sake*, will receive a hundredfold and will inherit eternal life. (Matthew 19:29)

> *For they have gone out for the sake of the name*, accepting nothing from the Gentiles. (3 John 1:7)

> I know you are enduring patiently and *bearing up for my name's sake*, and you have not grown weary. (Revelation 2:3)

That's why holy people speak the way they do:

> Your name will be magnified forever, [and people will always say], "The LORD of hosts is God over Israel,"

and the house of your servant David will be established before you. (2 Samuel 7:26)

In Judah God is known;
   his name is great in Israel. (Psalm 76:1)

Let them praise *the name of the LORD,*
   for his name alone is exalted;
      his majesty is above earth and heaven. (Psalm 148:13)

Your name, O LORD, endures forever,
   your renown, O LORD, throughout all ages.
      (Psalm 135:13)

And you will say in that day,

   "Give thanks to the LORD,
         call upon his name,
      make known his deeds among the peoples,
         proclaim that his name is exalted." (Isaiah 12:4)

Finally, Scripture says even judgment and God's execution of justice against the wicked is for His name's sake:

For this time I will send all my plagues on you yourself, and on your servants and your people, *so that you may know that there is none like me in all the earth.* (Exodus 9:14)

You saw the affliction of our fathers in Egypt and heard their cry at the Red Sea, and performed signs and wonders against Pharaoh and all his servants and all the people of his land, for you knew that they acted arrogantly against our fathers. *And you made a name for yourself, as it is to this day.* (Nehemiah 9:9-10)

To Make Him Known

The Bible also says God created the world to make Himself known, to communicate His perfections and excellence. This mirrors the things seen in the last chapter about His glory. Old Testament writers apparently held this view because they used it to explain what was awful about death: that one could no longer know or declare the works of God.

> Do you work wonders for the dead?
>   Do the departed rise up to praise you?
> Is your steadfast love declared in the grave,
>   or your faithfulness in Abaddon?
> *Are your wonders known in the darkness,*
>   *or your righteousness in the land of forgetfulness?*
>   (Psalm 88:10-12)

The same argument is used in Psalm 30:9 and Isaiah 38:18-19. In summary, the thing that makes death tragic is the same thing that makes life meaningful: knowing God and making Him known.

When the psalmist explains the consequences of creating the material universe in the first place, he links it to this idea:

> The heavens *declare* the glory of God,
>   and the sky above *proclaims* his handiwork.
> Day to day *pours out speech*,
>   and night to night *reveals knowledge*. (Psalm 19:1-2)

And when describing the purpose of God's providential acts in general, Scripture says,

> For to the snow he says, "Fall on the earth,"
>   likewise to the downpour, his mighty downpour.

He seals up the hand of every man,
 that all men whom he made may know it. (Job 37:6-7)

God explains the ultimate aim of all He created, saying,

The wild beasts will honor me,
 the jackals and the ostriches,
for I give water in the wilderness,
 rivers in the desert,
to give drink to my chosen people,
 the people whom I formed for myself
that they might declare my praise. (Isaiah 43:20-21)

And Peter encourages Christians to remember,

But you are a chosen race, a royal priesthood, a holy
nation, a people for his own possession, *that you may
proclaim the excellencies of him who called you out of
darkness into his marvelous light.* (1 Peter 2:9)

The desire to be known explains the logic behind all of the ordi-
nances and customs which God integrated into His redemptive
plan:

I will consecrate the tent of meeting and the altar.
Aaron also and his sons I will consecrate to serve me as
priests. I will dwell among the people of Israel and will
be their God. *And they shall know that I am the LORD
their God,* who brought them out of the land of Egypt
that I might dwell among them. I am the LORD their
God. (Exodus 29:44-46)

You are to speak to the people of Israel and say, "Above
all you shall keep my Sabbaths, for this is a sign

between me and you throughout your generations, *that you may know that I, the LORD, sanctify you."* (Exodus 31:13)

Continuing with this theme of "making God known," we might ask why God intervened in history with miracles. Here's how Scripture explains that:

Thus says the LORD, "*By this you shall know that I am the LORD*: behold, with the staff that is in my hand I will strike the water that is in the Nile, and it shall turn into blood." (Exodus 7:17)

Moses said, "Be it as you say, *so that you may know that there is no one like the LORD our God."* (Exodus 8:10)

I have led you forty years in the wilderness. Your clothes have not worn out on you, and your sandals have not worn off your feet. You have not eaten bread, and you have not drunk wine or strong drink, *that you may know that I am the LORD your God.* (Deuteronomy 29:5-6)

On that day your mouth will be opened to the fugitive, and you shall speak and be no longer mute. So you will be a sign to them, *and they will know that I am the LORD.* (Ezekiel 24:27)

And why does God have a redemptive plan to show mercy and favor to His people in the first place?

So now, O LORD our God, save us, please, from his hand, *that all the kingdoms of the earth may know that you, O LORD, are God alone.* (2 Kings 19:19)

When God rescued the Israelites from Egypt, He did so to make Himself known:

> Yet he saved them for his name's sake,
>> *that he might make known his mighty power.*
>>> (Psalm 106:8)

And when He stepped in to relieve from them the burden of their captivity in Babylon, God said,

> I will make you pass under the rod, and I will bring you into the bond of the covenant. I will purge out the rebels from among you, and those who transgress against me. I will bring them out of the land where they sojourn, but they shall not enter the land of Israel. Then you will know that I am the LORD. . . .
>
> *And you shall know that I am the LORD*, when I bring you into the land of Israel, the country that I swore to give to your fathers. . . . *And you shall know that I am the LORD*, when I deal with you for my name's sake, not according to your evil ways, nor according to your corrupt deeds, O house of Israel, declares the Lord GOD. (Ezekiel 20:37-38,42,44)

Not only was this God's purpose in redeeming Israel, but He planned all along to redeem the Gentiles for the same reason. He explains His missionary motivation in Isaiah:

> Thus says the Lord GOD:

> "Behold, I will lift up my hand to the nations,
>> and raise my signal to the peoples;

and they shall bring your sons in their arms,
 and your daughters shall be carried on their shoulders.
Kings shall be your foster fathers,
 and their queens your nursing mothers.
With their faces to the ground they shall bow down
  to you,
 and lick the dust of your feet.
Then you will know that I am the LORD;
 those who wait for me shall not be put to shame."
  (49:22-23)

A multitude of camels shall cover you,
 the young camels of Midian and Ephah;
 all those from Sheba shall come.
They shall bring gold and frankincense,
 and *shall bring good news, the praises of the LORD.* (60:6)

I will set a sign among them. And from them I will
send survivors to the nations, to Tarshish, Pul, and
Lud, who draw the bow, to Tubal and Javan, to the
coastlands far away, that have not heard my fame or
seen my glory. *And they shall declare my glory among
the nations.* (66:19)

In fact, this longing to know and make God known seems
to be the real fruit of holiness, and people who truly desire
to be in relationship with God are always depicted with these
desires too:

Oh give thanks to the LORD; call upon his name;
 make known his deeds among the peoples!
  (1 Chronicles 16:8)

> Sing to the Lord, all the earth!
> *Tell of his salvation* from day to day.
> *Declare his glory* among the nations,
>   his marvelous works among all the peoples!
>   (1 Chronicles 16:23-24)

In the fullness of time, God planned to complete His plan of redemption by sending Christ, the purpose of which Scripture describes in many places:

> God put [Him] forward as a propitiation by his blood, to be received by faith. *This was to show God's righteousness*, because in his divine forbearance he had passed over former sins. It was to show his righteousness at the present time, so that he might be just and the justifier of the one who has faith in Jesus. (Romans 3:25-26)

> But God, being rich in mercy, because of the great love with which he loved us, even when we were dead in our trespasses, made us alive together with Christ— by grace you have been saved—and raised us up with him and seated us with him in the heavenly places in Christ Jesus, *so that in the coming ages he might show the immeasurable riches of his grace in kindness toward us in Christ Jesus.* (Ephesians 2:4-7)

> To me, though I am the very least of all the saints, this grace was given, to preach to the Gentiles the unsearchable riches of Christ, and to bring to light for everyone what is the plan of the mystery hidden for ages in God who created all things, *so that through the church the manifold wisdom of God might now be made*

known to the rulers and authorities in the heavenly places. (Ephesians 3:8-10)

Save me from the mouth of the lion!
You have rescued me from the horns of the wild oxen!

I will tell of your name to my brothers;
in the midst of the congregation I will praise you.
(Psalm 22:21-22)

Oh that you would rend the heavens and come down,
    that the mountains might quake at your presence—
as when fire kindles brushwood
    and the fire causes water to boil—
to make your name known to your adversaries,
    and that the nations might tremble at your presence!
(Isaiah 64:1-2)

I made known to them your name, and I will continue to
make it known, that the love with which you have loved me may be in them, and I in them. (John 17:26)

Finally, God planned to make Himself known by purging the world of the wicked and punishing those who attempted to thwart His plan to communicate Himself. In fact, the "day of judgment" (Matthew 12:36) is also referred to as the "day of wrath when God's righteous judgment will be *revealed*" (Romans 2:5). Even in this purge, this judgment, God's nature is revealed and communicated. Several texts make this point:

But for this purpose I have raised you up, to show you my power, *so that my name may be proclaimed in all the earth.* (Exodus 9:16)

And you saw the affliction of our fathers in Egypt and heard their cry at the Red Sea, and performed signs and wonders against Pharaoh and all his servants and all the people of his land, for you knew that they acted arrogantly against our fathers. *And you made a name for yourself*, as it is to this day. (Nehemiah 9:9-10)

So He Would Be Praised

To wrap up, let's consider one last expression the Bible uses to explain *why God created the world*: to bring Him praise. Because we have already looked at several other expressions, I won't need to spend quite as long here, but there are nonetheless a few noteworthy passages that use this expression to answer our question.

They said to him, "Do you hear what these are saying?" And Jesus said to them, "Yes; have you never read,

"'Out of the mouth of infants and nursing babies
    you have prepared praise'?" (Matthew 21:16)

Praise for God is described as both the root and fruit of virtue:

So that you may approve what is excellent, and so be pure and blameless for the day of Christ, filled with the fruit of righteousness that comes through Jesus Christ, *to the glory and praise of God.* (Philippians 1:10-11)

God says He redeems and forgives to this end:

I will cleanse them from all the guilt of their sin against me, and I will forgive all the guilt of their sin and rebellion against me. *And this city shall be to me a name*

*of joy, a praise and a glory before all the nations of the
earth who shall hear of all the good that I do for them.*
They shall fear and tremble because of all the good and
all the prosperity I provide for it. (Jeremiah 33:8-9)

And we find these words constantly on the lips of those people
whom the Bible holds up as examples:

"Hallelujah! Praise the Lord! Praise Him forever!"

Conclusion

These expressions work together to explain the same idea from
different angles. They show that one isn't reading things into the
text when one sees God's glory, His name, His communication
of His own perfections, and His praise at the heart of His plan.
I think I have made my point on this issue, so now let's turn for
a minute to consider the way humanity and its interests fit into
all this from a biblical perspective.

DISCUSSION QUESTIONS

1. Edwards mentions three other expressions in this chapter that
   correspond to the idea of God glorifying Himself. What are they?
   Have you ever made the same connection that he made by
   thinking about them as "glory"?

2. The psalmist asks God to forgive him of his guilt for God's
   "name's sake." Why would God do such a thing? How does
   forgiveness affect the way we think about His "name"?

3. Have you ever done something with the explicit goal of "making
   God known" (that is, forgiving someone who didn't deserve

it, accepting an injustice to help someone else, and so on)? Is there a situation you're currently facing in which you could do so?

4. In his first letter, Peter reminds his readers, "You are a chosen race, a royal priesthood, a holy nation, a people for his own possession, that you may proclaim the excellencies of him who called you out of darkness into his marvelous light" (1 Peter 2:9). Can you remember the first time you realized that proclamation was a core component of the life of a Christian?

5. What does it mean for you to "proclaim the excellencies" of God in the different spheres of your life?

CHAPTER FIVE

His Daily Delight: God's Love for Humanity

The LORD is merciful and gracious, slow to anger and abounding in steadfast love.

PSALM 103:8

At the very beginning of this book, I introduced a few distinctions about goals. The first described the difference in means and ends, and the second described the difference between everyday pleasures and the most important objectives in our lives. To recap, I said God's highest goal was to expand His own goodness, truth, and beauty. Then I said that creating and knowing humanity—while not His highest goal—was nonetheless a pure goal, something He savors for its own sake.

This has an important implication. It means that God's mission to spread His own glory does not negate His enjoyment of humanity as an end unto itself. His love for you is not simply a tool for another project. You may not have been convinced that it is logically feasible to hold these two tensions together, so I addressed the idea specifically in the chapter on logical objections. But now that we have done a very robust search through

Scripture to understand God's highest goal—multiplying His essence and glory—I want to go back to this question about humanity. Does Scripture argue that God loves us purely, that we are an end unto ourselves? Or does it say that His affection for us is constantly clouded by a blind desire for some kind of dictatorial ego cult?

I think we will find that Scripture holds these two tensions together. God puts His glory first, but one of the primary ways He pours out His glory is in a pure love toward us. He communicates His nature powerfully and graciously in the context of relationship, and I hope seeing this from many angles in the Bible's pages will help bring these two ideas together in your mind the way God has done in history.

Preferring Mercy

When mankind rebels and tries to sabotage the good plans God has to expand His goodness, truth, and beauty, God intervenes. And occasionally we do hear Him talk about this punishment as a kind of goal, on the way toward restoring what has been corrupted:

> And as the LORD took delight in doing you good and multiplying you, so the LORD will take delight in bringing ruin upon you and destroying you. And you shall be plucked off the land that you are entering to take possession of it. (Deuteronomy 28:63)

> Thus shall my anger spend itself, and I will vent my fury upon them and satisfy myself. And they shall know that I am the LORD—that I have spoken in my jealousy—when I spend my fury upon them. (Ezekiel 5:13)

But the context of even these passages shows that God does not desire these things for their own sake, as if the misery and punishment of those He created comes naturally, or without reluctance on His part. In fact, many texts show that this punishment is merely a preliminary or lesser kind of goal and that God always prefers mercy:

> Say to them, As I live, declares the Lord GOD, *I have no pleasure in the death of the wicked, but that the wicked turn from his way and live;* turn back, turn back from your evil ways, for why will you die, O house of Israel? (Ezekiel 33:11)

> Who is a God like you, pardoning iniquity
>   and passing over transgression
>   for the remnant of his inheritance?
> *He does not retain his anger forever,*
>   *because he delights in steadfast love.* (Micah 7:18)

> They refused to obey and were not mindful of the wonders that you performed among them, but they stiffened their neck and appointed a leader to return to their slavery in Egypt. *But you are a God ready to forgive, gracious and merciful, slow to anger and abounding in steadfast love,* and did not forsake them. (Nehemiah 9:17)

> The LORD is merciful and gracious,
>   slow to anger and abounding in steadfast love.
>   (Psalm 103:8)

> *For he does not afflict from his heart*
>   or grieve the children of men. (Lamentations 3:33)

The Lord is not slow to fulfill his promise as some count slowness, but is patient toward you, *not wishing that any should perish, but that all should reach repentance.* (2 Peter 3:9)

Giving Grace for Its Own Sake

The Bible says that God gives grace gladly and that He is moved by the beauty of the story of redemption even more than we are. He indulges in forgiving us and sees the benefit of goodness to us for its own sake, not *simply* as a means to further ends. We see that nowhere more strongly than in these words from Deuteronomy:

It was not because you were more in number than any other people that the LORD set his love on you and chose you, for you were the fewest of all peoples, *but it is because the LORD loves you and is keeping the oath that he swore to your fathers*, that the LORD has brought you out with a mighty hand and redeemed you from the house of slavery, from the hand of Pharaoh king of Egypt. (7:7-8)

And the theme continues with more passages that talk about how goodness and mercy seem valuable on their own account:

Nevertheless, in your great mercies you did not make an end of them or forsake them, *for you are a gracious and merciful God.* (Nehemiah 9:31)

Remember not the sins of my youth or my transgressions;
    according to your steadfast love remember me,
    for the sake of your goodness, O LORD! (Psalm 25:7)

Loving Us Personally

This same theme of goodness for its own sake gets even more personal with the coming of Christ and His mission. Scripture says that Christ's mission flows not simply out of a utilitarian strategy, but out of a personal love and affection from God to His children:

> For God *so loved the world*, that he gave his only Son, that whoever believes in him should not perish but have eternal life. (John 3:16)

> But God, being rich in mercy, *because of the great love with which he loved us* . . . (Ephesians 2:4)

> In this the love of God was made manifest among us, that God sent his only Son into the world, so that we might live through him. In this is love, *not that we have loved God but that he loved us* and sent his Son to be the propitiation for our sins. (1 John 4:9-10)

He lived and suffered on the cross and was resurrected not for a principle but for people whom He loved in a direct, personal way. You cannot read the Bible's words about God's motives and think that His desire to glorify Himself left Him without true and abiding passion for us, the products of His glory:

> I have been crucified with Christ. It is no longer I who live, but Christ who lives in me. And the life I now live in the flesh I live by faith in the Son of God, *who loved me and gave himself for me.* (Galatians 2:20)

> Husbands, love your wives, *as Christ loved the church and gave himself up for her.* (Ephesians 5:25)

I am praying for them. I am not praying for the world but for those whom you have given me, *for they are yours.* (John 17:9)

When Isaiah talks about the coming Messiah and the Messiah's mission, he makes it clear that that figure will see His redemptive work as a true goal or prize, a pure goal in which He will be satisfied:

Yet it was the will of the LORD to crush him;
    he has put him to grief;
when his soul makes an offering for guilt,
    he shall see his offspring; he shall prolong his days;
the will of the LORD shall prosper in his hand.
Out of the anguish of his soul *he shall see and be satisfied;*
by his knowledge shall the righteous one, my servant,
    make many to be accounted righteous,
    and he shall bear their iniquities. (Isaiah 53:10-11)

A bit later Isaiah expresses the same idea again:

For as a young man marries a young woman,
    so shall your sons marry you,
and *as the bridegroom rejoices over the bride,*
    so shall your God rejoice over you. (Isaiah 62:5)

Other Old Testament texts describe scenes that are just as vivid:

The LORD your God is in your midst,
    a mighty one who will save;
he will rejoice over you with gladness;
    he will quiet you by his love;
he will exult over you with loud singing. (Zephaniah 3:17)

> Then I was beside him, like a master workman,
> *and I was daily his delight,*
> rejoicing before him always,
> rejoicing in his inhabited world
> and delighting in the children of man.
> (Proverbs 8:30-31)

Making Virtue Humane

In contrast to the brutal codes of conduct common to so many ancient societies, Scripture's teaching was permeated by an inherently high view of humanity. This stemmed from God's own view, that mankind was sacred because it carried His image. Other ancient views embodied a kind of harsh indifference to humanity's circumstances, because the gods they worshipped were depicted as acting this way toward humanity. But in God's plan, love and care for *one another*—behaviors rooted in God's own love and care for you and me—become the hallmarks of true Christian virtue. One hears this view in texts such as this:

> Owe no one anything, except to love each other, for the one who loves another has fulfilled the law. For the commandments, "You shall not commit adultery, You shall not murder, You shall not steal, You shall not covet," and any other commandment, are summed up in this word: "You shall love your neighbor as yourself." Love does no wrong to a neighbor; *therefore love is the fulfilling of the law*. (Romans 13:8-10)

> For the whole law is fulfilled in one word: "You shall *love* your neighbor as yourself." (Galatians 5:14)

If you really fulfill the royal law according to the Scripture, "You shall love your neighbor as yourself," you are doing well. (James 2:8)

Designing Systems with Us in Mind

Instead of seeing mankind as the captive of a legalistic universe, Scripture in general, and Jesus in particular, argue that the systems and customs God passed down were made to serve us and work for our good, not the other way around. This explains Christ's famous reply to the Pharisees:

And he said to them, "*The Sabbath was made for man, not man for the Sabbath.* So the Son of Man is lord even of the Sabbath." (Mark 2:27-28)

Christ makes this point here about the Sabbath, but He grounds His rationale in His own lordship. What does this imply? That for all things over which He is Lord, the same principle applies. Not only should we see ourselves as liberated from the mechanistic view of the world the Pharisees took regarding the purpose of the Jewish Sabbath, we should see ourselves as liberated from such views in all of reality. Christ, after all, is not only lord of the Sabbath but Lord of everything. So when we hear that He is seated at God's right hand, the King of angels and men, the Head of the universe, and vested with all power and authority, we should rest assured that He is constantly using that authority for our good.

Interceding to Rescue Us

After the Fall, God cursed the earth so that we might never again mistake it for the place He desired it to be for us. The natural world reminds us of this on a regular basis. But because of God's faithfulness to us and sovereignty over all He has created, we regularly hear Him talk about acting in the material world and overcoming the limitations of the curse to come to rescue us. This happened in the hundreds of miracles Scripture records, but several mental images sum it up perhaps even better. In Deuteronomy, for example, Moses says to Jeshurun,

> There is none like God, O Jeshurun,
>> *who rides through the heavens to your help,*
>> through the skies in his majesty. (33:26)

And in another powerful image, Ezekiel sees a great throne seated on earth which depicts God as the absolute ruler of all history and circumstances. This vision reminds us that God is not weak and He has not lost control over the creation which often seems to be lost to evil:

> Over the heads of the living creatures there was the likeness of an expanse, shining like awe-inspiring crystal, spread out above their heads. . . . And above the expanse over their heads there was the likeness of a throne, in appearance like sapphire; and seated above the likeness of a throne was a likeness with a human appearance. And upward from what had the appearance of his waist I saw as it were gleaming metal, like the appearance of fire enclosed all around. And downward from what had the appearance of his waist I saw as it were the appearance of fire, and there was brightness around him. Like the appearance of the bow that is in the cloud on the day of rain, so was the appearance of the brightness all around.

> *Such was the appearance of the likeness of the glory*
> *of the LORD. And when I saw it, I fell on my face.*
> (Ezekiel 1:22,26-28)

Vindicating the Oppressed

The Bible says God's battle against those who oppress His people is also meant for their happiness:

> For I am the LORD your God,
>   the Holy One of Israel, your Savior.
> I give Egypt as your ransom,
>   Cush and Seba in exchange for you.
> *Because you are precious in my eyes,*
>   *and honored, and I love you,*
> *I give men in return for you,*
>   *peoples in exchange for your life.* (Isaiah 43:3-4)

It says He will one day vindicate all those who have been left at the mercy of evil people. In an incredible refrain about God's love, the psalmist goes through dozens of different events in which it has been made manifest, and among them he lists all those from whom God delivered His people:

> [He] struck down the firstborn of Egypt,
>   for his steadfast love endures forever;
> and brought Israel out from among them,
>   for his steadfast love endures forever; . . .
> but overthrew Pharaoh and his host in the Red Sea,
>   for his steadfast love endures forever; . . .
>
> [He] who struck down great kings,
>   for his steadfast love endures forever;

and killed mighty kings,
>for his steadfast love endures forever;
Sihon, king of the Amorites,
>for his steadfast love endures forever;
and Og, king of Bashan,
>for his steadfast love endures forever.
>>(Psalm 136:10-11,15,17-20)

Offering a Share of Everything

God alone created the world, and yet Scripture often speaks of it as if it belongs to us, too. This is another sign of the goodness and favor we have in God's eyes. For example, consider Paul's words to the Corinthians:

> So let no one boast in men. For all things are yours, whether Paul or Apollos or Cephas or the world or life or death or the present or the future—all are yours.
> (1 Corinthians 3:21-22)

Now, in the truest sense, everything belongs to God, who created the world, so what's the intent here? I think the most natural sense is the very one we have been tracing all along, that everything is made for our benefit. This means we should count human wisdom, and its use of the world around it, as foolishness in comparison with the use which God has in mind for it, to bless us by glorifying Himself.

Working for Our Good

Not only is the whole created world offered to us, the Bible claims that God's providence and action in history always serve our good. This theme starts in the Old Testament, in texts such as:

> To him who alone does great wonders,
> for his steadfast love endures forever;
> to him who by understanding made the heavens,
> for his steadfast love endures forever;
> to him who spread out the earth above the waters,
> for his steadfast love endures forever;
> to him who made the great lights,
> for his steadfast love endures forever;
> the sun to rule over the day,
> for his steadfast love endures forever;
> the moon and stars to rule over the night,
> for his steadfast love endures forever.
> (Psalm 136:4-9)

And it continues very powerfully in words from Paul such as:

> And we know that *for those who love God all things work together for good*, for those who are called according to his purpose. (Romans 8:28)

Planning from All Eternity

Finally, Jesus' words about the end of the world lead us to believe that God began His plan for humanity with the end in mind. In Matthew, He tells us what the righteous will hear at the end of time:

> Then the King will say to those on his right, "Come, you who are blessed by my Father, inherit the kingdom

prepared for you from the foundation of the world."
(Matthew 25:34)

This means that God's goodness to us now is simply one instance of His eternal expression of favor.

Conclusion

Over and over in this book, we have seen two ideas woven together: first, that God's highest priority is to expand Himself into all reaches of reality; and second, that this priority means great things for you, me, and the rest of humanity. I think it would be fitting to conclude this book by noting one last tension, perhaps the most beautiful tension in the whole idea: that there will never come a day when the process is truly complete.

We intuit this fact sometimes when we think about the problem of evil. God tries to fulfill what justice demands by separating Himself from sinners forever in hell, and because this separates good from evil *forever*, it accomplishes justice's goal. At the same time, there will never be a moment when justice has been perfectly satisfied, when evil has been so punished that the legacy of its destruction seems totally compensated for.

Yet on the other side of things, we should think about God's pursuit of goodness, of truth, and of beauty with just the same tension. That is, God could have easily stopped with the creation of the physical universe itself and have outdone what anyone in history has created or ever will create. So what keeps Him going? The same thing which led Him to create in the first place and which will drive Him to unfathomable new heights well into the eternal horizon: His desire to expand His nature, to glorify His name, first for its own sake but second for the joy it gives to us who know and get to experience relationship with Him.

Both Scripture and logic have presented a picture of God, and of the story He started with us, that transcend anything we could have devised on our own. And that's the point. You and I are invited into a story bigger than us, older than us, and more beautiful than us. It was grace which began the story, and it was grace which rescued us from our sabotage of His good plan. That, I hope you will now be able to see, is why Peter prayed, "To him be the glory both now and to the day of eternity" (2 Peter 3:18).

DISCUSSION QUESTIONS

1. Edwards starts off quoting a couple of texts that speak strongly about God's judgment, but he says the context of those passages, and passages elsewhere, show that God does not *what*?

2. At one point in the chapter, Edwards says God shows His love for us by His willingness to intercede to rescue us. Has there ever been a time in your life in which you have experienced this in an especially powerful way?

3. Among the ways we know that God loves us, Edwards says that He vindicates the oppressed. Is there a particular subset of the world's oppressed people that He has put specifically on your heart?

4. Edwards shares many different motifs in Scripture that argue for God's personal love for us. Can you explain two of those in your own words?

5. According to this chapter, what is the root of the Bible's command that we love one another? Does that make it easier for you to follow?

CHAPTER SIX

Practical Considerations

In the original concluding chapter of his book, Edwards surveyed all of the different ideas he had covered in parts 1 and 2. I have done that in the appendix called "Using This Book for Small-Group Study." I will give you a couple of the condensed arguments in this chapter as well, and I wove his very last thoughts into the conclusion of part 2, chapter 5. But I feel like it would be helpful to wrap up this adaptation of such an old, lofty book not by fixating on how old and lofty it is, but by showing how incredibly practical and productive these ideas can be today, even or especially in non-Christian contexts. That may seem like an abrupt transition from the subject matter we covered in the book, but for people considering whether Christianity makes sense, few questions have more relevance than why God created the world. Let me explain how that can play out in real life.

As I mentioned in the introduction, my wife and I live in

Berlin, Germany, which sociologist Peter Berger has called the "world capital of atheism." And as a theologian here, I spend the majority of my time answering these two questions: (1) What does Christianity *say* history is about? and (2) Is its explanation of history actually *true*? These are two completely independent questions, and the more I'm able to keep them separate, the more productive my conversations are. Why? Because you will never have a worthwhile debate about whether Jesus' ideas are *true* if you haven't first defined what Jesus' ideas *are*.

So, whenever I have the chance to talk about Christianity with people, I always go for that first question. I ask them to allow themselves to think about the gospel like a novel or screenplay, to decide whether they think the story is internally coherent, before trying to decide whether it's true. Almost without exception, people seem more at ease talking about it from this perspective. For them, it means getting to engage with the plot of the gospel like they do with the last movie they saw, instead of like a winner-takes-all philosophical debate. And for me, it means getting to explain all the gripping and moving aspects of the story without having to have first made the case that they're true. This, I should note, usually changes the tone of any conversation about truth we might have later anyway.

What does all of this have to do with why God created the world? Well, if you want to talk with your friends about the coherency of the Christian explanation of history and connect the dots in a way that makes the story sound logical, almost nothing is more thought-provoking than unpacking God's rationale for creating something in the first place. It explains the overarching plot and therefore the main conflict as well. It makes the Fall, even as a literary device, seem tragic and foolish.

If you understand why God created the world, then you understand what makes something good, what makes something evil, why we worship God, and why it makes no sense to worship anything else. God's motive for creation is the piece of the story that gives tension to all the other parts.

In my experience, non-Christians find the question we discussed in this book interesting for an entirely different reason than Christians might: the seeming lack of a logical answer appears itself to constitute an argument against Christianity. I occasionally highlight that problem, knowing that it's a perceived weak point. I might mention the popular answers for why God created us (egomania, loneliness, and so on) to talk about why they don't work, just to make sure they understand that I'm on the same page with them. This builds up tension and interest about the answer I have, and such tension just makes the conversation that much more engaging.

Explaining the Idea Quickly

You can segue to why God created the world from almost any part of a conversation about religion or Christianity by saying, "I think the Bible's explanation of why God created the world helps make a bit of sense out of this issue." But even if you get to that point, how do you explain Edwards's answer quickly enough that you don't lose momentum? Well, you'll have to put it in your own words and in a way that feels seamless with the particular conversation you're in, but I think you should try to keep three ideas in mind. The ideas build on one another in such a way as to bring the topic to life pretty quickly.

First, explain why it doesn't make sense to think God was trying to fulfill a need.

If the universe couldn't offer anything that God didn't already have before creation, then He must not have created to fulfill a need. Instead, He must have created because of the way it promoted something He valued, something good, true, or beautiful.

Everything that exists came from God's hand, so the universe isn't an answer to material needs. And because of the Trinity, we have reason to believe that God had fulfilling relationships without us. So instead of trying to fulfill a need, it seems more likely that He was trying to accomplish or promote something, something which I have summarized with the classic triad "the good, true, and beautiful."

Second, help them connect the dots with this question: *"What existed before the creation of the world that was good, true, and beautiful?"*

This is the key. Once it becomes obvious that the things we love now, in the created world, are all just God diffused—that at one time everything we love and which inspires us was entirely pent up in a single being—our view of God can never be the same. You can build on this epiphany in different ways, but the important thing is to show how the answer makes *sense* of God's decision to create and *nonsense* out of our subsequent attempts to be for ourselves and others what only He can be.

Third and last, talk about how God's priority of expanding His glory (see part 2, chapter 3) works out for our good as well. You might use the example of a diamond, which I mentioned in part 1, chapter 4:

"There is no dichotomy between a diamond's desire to sparkle and the sun's desire to shine. In fact, from the point of view of the diamond, these two goals are inseparable. When you rush to see a shiny new diamond on someone's finger, you are in fact, knowingly or unknowingly, rushing to admire how beautiful the light can be

when seen through a vessel made specifically to reflect it well. And the diamond you find on that finger will be beautiful only insofar as the sun shines brightly. . . . In the same way, God's expansion into all reaches of reality is directly bound up with our search for love, joy, and profundity. These things are only found in Him, and they will only ever be found in us, and in our experience, to the extent that He Himself is in us and in our experience."

If your conversations about this topic work out like mine have, your friends will immediately respond by saying, "Well, that sounds great, but that's not the way the world actually is. Where is all of God's goodness, truth, and beauty now?" This is essentially a request to explain the fall of mankind, and since they understand God's aim in creation, that should be an easy next step. In summary, we have rejected God's attempts to try to fill us and the world with His essence and have instead tried to find and produce those things ourselves. That explains the destruction and emptiness we see around us. "So what plan does God have to fix *that* problem?" If you make it that far in the conversation, you will probably find yourself talking about the Cross before long.

Conclusion

Over the last few centuries, Christians have had a great track record of doing what you might call "philosophical apologetics," of talking about the question of truth. We have done lots of great research into epistemology, historiography, theism, and issues related to the Resurrection. These are strengths we have to hold on to and which the modern world demands of us. For our own spiritual edification, we have also made a great deal of progress in understanding the story's contours, using things like "biblical theology," and this has helped *us* see how the Bible fits together.

What we haven't done as much, perhaps, is to take the lessons of biblical theology, all of that material we have gathered about how the story works, and used it apologetically, as a kind of "theological apologetics." We haven't thought to combine apologetics and biblical theology in a way that lets people consider the story's coherency on its own merits first, before debating whether it's true. That is exactly where Edwards has such a gift to offer us. He dug deep into Scripture to understand not only *what* God has done but also *why* He has done it, why it makes amazing sense. And there are few things the world needs more than lucid answers to these "why?" questions of the Christian story.

To conclude, therefore, I would simply encourage you to put these ideas to use. They're not just for late-night chats between theologians, but also for late-night chats with people trying to wrap their minds around the gospel for the first time. Draw them in on this issue. The intrigue is there. The tension is there. What an interesting launching point for a skeptic to start chipping away at his questions. It's surprising how eerily plausible the whole story becomes once you understand why God created the world.

Using This Book for Small-Group Study

I had a great time uncovering all that Edwards packed into this book, but I think it would have been much more enjoyable to have done so in a group setting. As such, I tried to think ahead about groups that would read the text together. Each chapter comes with a few discussion questions to get you started, and I have made a short overview of the chapters below so leaders can get a feel for the material at a glance.

As you may have already noticed, Edwards's ideas go fairly deep fairly quickly, so some people may need extra time to reflect and ask questions. For that reason, I would suggest the following strategy for dividing up the material into a typical eight-week group study:

Week 1: Introduction and Part 1, Chapter 1
Week 2: Part 1, Chapter 2
Week 3: Part 1, Chapters 3–4
Week 4: Part 1, Chapter 5
Week 5: Part 2, Chapters 1–2
Week 6: Part 2, Chapters 3–4
Week 7: Part 2, Chapters 5–6
Week 8: Appendix B, Wrap-Up

However your group decides to split up the content, I hope it will be as powerful and positive an experience for you as it was for me when I first encountered the material. Thanks for considering this book for your next group study!

Chapter Overviews

PART I: LOGIC

CHAPTER 1: MOTIVES: A FEW HELPFUL DISTINCTIONS

We want to discuss God's motives for creating the world, and motives can be hard to quantify. This chapter, therefore, will give us some vocabulary for the discussion and introduce the categories we will use to find an answer to our question.

CHAPTER 2: GOOD, TRUE, AND BEAUTIFUL: FIRST STEPS TOWARD AN ANSWER

If God does not need, and cannot receive, anything new from something He creates, then He must not have created in order to fill a need. And if creation does not arise to fulfill some need that God has, then it must arise because of the way it accomplishes something that He values. Chapter 2 builds on this idea to explain the book's most basic, logical thesis.

CHAPTER 3: SET LOOSE: THE FRUITS OF CREATION

Whatever happened as a result of creation was God's goal. That's because God always accomplishes what He sets out to do. So as I thought about ways to check our thesis, I decided we should spend some time considering just that: What actually happened as a result of the creation of the world? Chapter 3 considers four interesting examples.

CHAPTER 4: ONE AND THE SAME: HOW WE FIT IN THE PLAN

Creation is the beginning of something external to God, so it may seem ironic that I have been suggesting *He* is the goal of creation. Wouldn't it make more sense, in light of this defini- tion, to think He might be making *others* the point? To clear up possible misunderstandings, chapter 4 talks about the relation- ship between God's self-expansion and the physical world.

CHAPTER 5: OBJECTIONS: EXAMINING GOD'S CHARACTER

To conclude the conversation about logic, I want to give some time and attention to those readers who have been frustrated with the thesis as I have presented it thus far. As I considered the content of the previous chapters, four major critiques came to mind that I might logically raise against the thesis myself. We spend chapter 5 considering those.

PART II: SCRIPTURE

CHAPTER 1: TO AND THROUGH AND FOR: THE CLEAR ANSWER IN SCRIPTURE

From the first page to the last page, Scripture says God put Himself at the center of His plan in creation. Chapter 1 shares a few well-known texts that make this point and explains my goal in part 2: to help remove any doubts or suspicions you might have about having been misled, or momentarily convinced of an extreme, one-sided view, by showing that the Bible takes this position from all sides. We also discuss where in the Bible we should go to find an answer to our question.

CHAPTER 2: A WORD AND A PROCESS: DEFINING THE WORD *GLORY*

The word *glory* is going to figure largely into the Bible's answers to our questions, and though many people will have heard this word before, they might have a hard time explaining exactly what it means. So chapter 2 takes a moment to look at how the Bible itself defines the word *glory*, first the term on its own and then the fascinating process that is usually implied with it.

CHAPTER 3: GLORY: GOD'S WORK IN HISTORY

Chapter 3 is the largest segment of part 2. It looks at Scripture's teaching on many different fronts and asks explicit questions about *why God created the world*. It also asks more general questions like why God created mankind, what He requires of us, what lies at the root of goodness and in the hearts of the saints, what motivated Christ during His mission, and what seems to motivate God's decisions on matters big and small.

CHAPTER 4: THEN YOU WILL KNOW: GLORY BY ANOTHER NAME

Chapter 3 showed how much the Bible uses the expression "God's glory." But there are many different turns of phrase and mental images which are used to convey the same idea, and each serves as a slightly different lens through which to look at the topic. To round out and complement what we said in the previous chapter, chapter 4 covers three more expressions the Bible uses to explain why God created the world.

CHAPTER 5: HIS DAILY DELIGHT: GOD'S LOVE FOR HUMANITY

In part 1, we spent some time discussing the logical reasons why God's mission to spread His own glory does not negate His enjoyment of humanity as an end unto itself. Chapter 5 goes back to Scripture with the same question, to see whether it argues that God loves us for our own sakes.

CHAPTER 6: PRACTICAL CONSIDERATIONS

In chapter 6, I show how helpful and exciting the ideas of the book can be when we use them to explain the gospel to non-Christian friends.

The Story of Jonathan Edwards

I am either the best or the worst person to tell the story of Jonathan Edwards. I came to this book project without knowing a great deal about him, and I haven't spent an inordinate amount of time in deep research about him since then. So, some of you probably know more about him than I do. On the other hand, I may be the best person to write about him because, as a newcomer to the topic, I started asking the same questions any ordinary person might have. And in the case of this particular man, that may be especially valuable. Why?

Before I knew anything about Jonathan Edwards's ideas, I knew that he had a fan club that transcended easy categorization. I once had a chance to audit part of a great course on his life and was shocked to hear that several people in the class had named their children Jonathan Edwards. Others had met their spouses at Jonathan Edwards reading clubs. This wasn't a school-wide phenomenon, and the course obviously attracted that crowd. But I confess it seemed (and still does seem) strange to me that some people went so far in their interest for him. I can't think of a parallel with any other figure in Christian history. Know anyone who met his or her spouse at a Thomas Aquinas reading club?

If I can speak as an outsider, I think this cloud of fans may explain some of why Edwards seems suspect to the uninitiated. The fan club occasionally implies that a person has to be fascinated with the man, his times, his rhetorical style, and all the trappings of his daily life, as a *prerequisite* to entering the world of his ideas. I didn't take that journey and so I can assure you: It isn't a prerequisite. Also, my research inclines me to believe that Edwards would have been discouraged by the thought of his biographical details overshadowing his theological contributions.

On the other hand, if I can speak as someone who has finally taken a closer look at Edwards's life, I can confidently say that it could be the subject of multiple feature films. That is, though he doesn't seem to have been the most socially dynamic person ever, he wore many different hats at a fascinating time in history, and the predicaments he encountered are enough to make his story engaging all by themselves. His occasionally brilliant solutions to those predicaments just enhance the effect. So I am now more sympathetic to the interest in his biography.

As I said in the introduction, there are many resources available for learning about his life. I loved the abridged version of George Marsden's biography, *Jonathan Edwards: A Life*, as well as Michael Reeves's sketch of him in *On Giants' Shoulders*. John Piper has great extended notes on Edwards in his (freely available) re-release of this book in its original text, *God's Passion for His Glory*. And I'm currently reading *The Essential Edwards Collection*, edited by Owen Strachan and Doug Sweeney, and Sam Storms's book *Signs of the Spirit*, a paraphrase of Edwards's *Religious Affections*. For the absolute purist, all of his original works are available at http://edwards.yale.edu/, where I first got my hands on this text.

Because those other resources exist and because the subject is so wide-reaching, I don't feel like I need to give a full sketch of his life. But because it's the multifaceted nature of his story which makes him so interesting, let me give you a bit of information on the most prominent angles. I'll leave you in the good hands of the authors I mentioned to fill in the details.

The Basics

Jonathan Edwards was born on October 5, 1703, in East Windsor, Connecticut, to Timothy Edwards and Esther Stoddard. He learned Latin at age six and went off to Yale at age fifteen, where he got both a bachelor's degree and an MA. Out of college, he interned and pastored in a few congregations, hoping to eventually be called to pastor in New York City. But that plan never worked out, and he spent the majority of his life in churches in rural Massachusetts. He met and married Sarah Pierrepont shortly after ending seminary, and over the course of their lives they had eleven children together. After a life of energetic scholarship and worship, he died on March 22, 1758, at the age of only fifty-four, due to a complication from a smallpox inoculation which he had organized for his family to receive.

In his comparatively short life, Edwards took part in an impressive variety of experiences and vocations. Let me highlight just a few of those, namely: that he was a British-American, a member of a powerful family, a God-centered convert, a prolific writer and theologian, a revival leader, an influential town pastor, a missionary to the Native Americans, and the president of Princeton University.

British-American

As George Marsden notes in his book, the story of Rip van Winkle is helpful for anyone trying to understand Edwards's life. Van Winkle was a fictitious character who slept through the American Revolution, and then was shocked by how life in his hometown had changed when he woke up twenty years later. Significantly for us, Edwards didn't live to see those changes. He was born and died before the revolution, in fact before it was even an option on the table. Though he lived in Massachusetts, he was categorically not a citizen of the *United States*, and he therefore belonged to that now-forgotten society which saw itself as an extension of England.

His grandfather came to the colonies forty years after the first settlers had and could still remember Oliver Cromwell and England's Glorious Revolution. That fact made Edwards's role in history a bit ironic. As a pastor, he played an important part in making sure that the establishment, and the ways of the Puritan fathers, stayed in power. Yet the Puritan fathers had themselves been some of the first modern revolutionaries and had gone to great lengths to overthrow the authorities of the day, even murdering their king.

At any rate, Edwards felt compelled to try to uphold the principles of his revolutionary forefathers, but he had no idea his descendants would be part of another revolution not long after his death, which would in some ways undermine the establishment the Puritans had created. And whatever he would have thought of the later revolution, we should remember that much of what we associate with "the American way of thinking and life" was not a part of his experience in the British colonies.

Member of a Powerful Family

Edwards's grandfather, pastor Solomon Stoddard, was the most powerful man in the western part of the colonies. His uncle, John Stoddard, was the most powerful government official in the region and served as judge, senator, and delegate to all kinds of assemblies. Increase and Cotton Mather, relatives on his mother's side, were the leading clergy in Boston, and when Edwards went to Yale at the age of fifteen, his cousin Elisha Williams was his official tutor. The legacy didn't end with him, though. His grandson, Aaron Burr, became the Vice President of the United States, and Burr was only one of many prominent descendants.

If one doesn't see the power simply in his family tree, one definitely hears it in the details of his life. As a wedding gift, Edwards reportedly received a large house, a barn, three acres of land in town, ten acres on the edge of town, and forty acres of land outside of town to be used for passive income. This was all in addition to a salary that was among the highest in the region for a pastor. None of this is to condemn Edwards, and as far as I can tell, he used both his influence and his financial means for the good of others. It's just interesting to note that this man, whom we think of like any other pastor, was a member of the aristocracy of his time, and that an awareness of this fact seemed to color his thinking.

God-Centered Convert

Jonathan Edwards lived in an age during which thinking people were trying to do for reality itself what Newton had done for physics: offer a unifying theory of everything. There was a kind of race to the finish line for intellectuals, and the prize went to the man who could show how all things were interrelated and wrapped up into a single story. While others tried to do this by using ideas from the Enlightenment, Edwards seems to have inadvertently stumbled onto a solution to the problem in his own religious convictions, specifically in God's nature and His sovereignty.

Though it turned out to be useful for his intellectual pursuits, Edwards had in fact been fascinated with the doctrine of God for its own sake since he was very young. Many of us wonder how it even dawned on him to write a book about why God created the world. That's because we start with our own existential problems and ask theological questions only insofar as they ease our concerns. At the risk of slightly oversimplifying things, it seems like Edwards often came at it the other way around. He conceived of things by starting with God and working toward himself (as in this book) rather than starting with humanity and working back toward God (as most of us naturally do).

All his life, his favorite hobby was walking through the woods, contemplating the ways that nature pointed toward a higher reality in God, and praying. In fact, his books were full of metaphors from these walks, like analogies about the light, trees, honey, and so forth. So, as one might expect, he found Scripture most interesting when it was talking about God's nature, as in one of his favorite texts, where Paul says:

> To the King of the ages, immortal, invisible, the only
> God, be honor and glory forever and ever. Amen.
> (1 Timothy 1:17)

Writer and Theologian

When Edwards went on his daily walks through the woods, he often pinned a blank scrap of paper to his jacket so that he would have a way to write down any thought that came to him. When the family hit hard times financially, some of his children started making ladies' fans for extra money, and Edwards stitched unused scraps of their paper together to make journals. He even had his Bible rebound with a slip of blank paper added between each page for taking notes. He always seemed to be on the lookout for a place to write down his ideas.

Of course, these notes weren't simply diary entries. They grew out of one of his primary life goals. Early on, he had made this commitment: "When I think of any theorem in divinity to be solved, [I will] immediately do what I can towards solving it, if circumstances do not hinder."[1] He felt a burden to offer coherent restatements of the logic of Christianity for his age, one of which—surprising though it may seem now—was experiencing a faith crisis. And whether one stands inside Edwards's Reformed tradition or not, I think we have to agree that Edwards was overwhelmingly faithful to his commitment. There are few topics which he didn't handle in writing, and in many cases the books speak to truly universal Christian concerns, as was the case in this one.

I'm just beginning to dive into the rest of these works myself, so I will refer you to the excellent summaries that people like John Piper and Michael Reeves give of them to get an informed overview. But Edwards tended to be most interested in the most difficult subjects, and even when his writing was more down-to-earth, it somehow still seemed a bit lofty. Just consider one

---

1 John Piper, *God's Passion for His Glory* (Wheaton: Crossway, 1998), xii.

of the volumes I came across in my research. Edwards gave it this memorable title: *An Humble Attempt to Promote Explicit Agreement and Visible Union of God's People thro' the World, in Extraordinary Prayer, for the Revival of Religion, and the Advancement of Christ's Kingdom on Earth, Pursuant to Scripture Promise and Prophecies Concerning the Last Times.*

Revival Leader

Most people today think of Jonathan Edwards primarily as a writer. But in his own era, he was arguably more famous as a revival leader, a man who inspired both John Wesley and George Whitefield, and who led an entire city through two all-encompassing awakenings. Edwards's grandfather was one of the first Puritans to hold regularly scheduled meetings to pray for revival, in his case about once a decade. He passed on this emphasis for renewal and conversion to his grandson Jonathan, and Jonathan experienced two major periods of revival himself, in 1735 and in 1742. These refined the way that he thought about and prayed for such visitations from God, and because he published books on them, they refined many others' thinking about revivals as well.

Edwards explained the need for revival of the heart, and for conversion, with one of his many nature metaphors: honey. It's one thing, he argued, to know or to have been told that honey is sweet. Yet it is a different thing to have personally tasted the sweetness of honey. A Christianized culture may be filled with people who have heard that honey is sweet who have, yet, never experienced its sweetness or been nourished by it. So he saw all of his own academic efforts as simply the seedbed for that most important experience of knowing God, and of *desiring God*, via true conversion.

While the first revival of Northampton was still going on, Edwards decided to write a report about it. The book became a bestseller both in the colonies and in Europe, where it inspired people like John Wesley and George Whitefield, preachers in the second revival in 1742, The Great Awakening. But all the fame this won for his town also showed Edwards how hard it is to accurately assess a revival in the heat of the moment. A number of the cases about which he had excitedly reported in his first book on revival, for example, turned out to have been just enthusiasm. The people returned to their old ways before long, and this left just as much of an impression on him as had the initial revival.

By the time the second major revival came along, Edwards had spent a lot of time thinking about the heart and about how to identify real conversions. These formed the basis of one of his most famous books, *Religious Affections*, and built on the kinds of cautions that Jesus had given in the parable of the Sower (see Matthew 13:1-9). I am myself only now getting into the work, but its focus on the heart does seem like the perfect complement to this book, in which he engaged the intellect so intensely.

Town Pastor

I have arranged these aspects of Edwards's life so that the longest and most defined seasons would come in chronological order. Let me start, then, with his pastorate. Because his plans didn't work out to go to New York after seminary, Edwards eventually became assistant pastor to his grandfather, Solomon Stoddard.

Stoddard had pastored The First Church of Northampton for nearly *sixty* years. During that time he had come up with several innovative practices and policies which his people saw as virtually scriptural ever after. Edwards enjoyed his work in the congregation, but when he became the lead pastor two years later, he realized that all of those years of innovating and experimenting by his grandfather would make his own role significantly more complicated.

Even though he loved studying in his office all day, the people of his church heard from him a lot. Like most of his peers, he preached for nearly two hours on Sundays, and he regularly held lectures in town. He didn't make many house calls to peoples' homes, but apparently people came calling on him instead. In spite of his reserved personality, he often had the ear of the whole town.

At the time he pastored, his town and his church were nearly one in the same. The church had 620 "full members," but his grandfather had supported the old parish system, in which every citizen is technically a member. That made Edwards much more than a simple congregation pastor. He was truly "the town pastor." Sometimes he carried the whole town on his shoulders into revival, and sometimes he became the object of the whole town's ridicule. This amplified the predicament that most pastors face, and after twenty-three years at his post, the high-stakes setup led the congregation, which had loved him so much, to dismiss him.

Two incidents paved the way for his dismissal. In the first, Edwards confronted (a bit clumsily) what was basically an eighteenth-century case of "sexting." Several single men in his congregation used graphic anatomy books to harass and embarrass single women, and Edwards would not let the issue rest, hoping to get their repentance and apologies. In the second case, Edwards confronted a church member who had impregnated a young woman without marrying her. The congregant, and his parents, thought that a cash payment to the young woman's poor family should be enough to make amends, but Edwards thought Christian principles dictated otherwise. Both of these cases dragged on for a long time, and many in the Northampton community thought they constituted unnecessary meddling in their affairs.

These issues might have been forgotten, but in a last issue of sacrilege, Edwards tried to revise his grandfather's policies on church membership by requiring a story of conversion from new members. The details of this incident are covered in almost all of the books I mentioned at the beginning of this bio, and it makes for intriguing reading. But suffice it to say, Edwards's grandfather's fan club saw the switch as high heresy and succeeded in forcibly removing him. At age forty-six, this left him jobless with a family of nine to support, and it would take a whole year before he was able to find other work and finally leave town.

Missionary to the Native Americans

Near the end of his pastorate, Edwards's family hosted a sick, young missionary named David Brainerd. Brainerd had made daring solo trips into the Pennsylvania wilderness to try to reach Native Americans in their villages. But the trips had taken their toll, and he had come down with a bad case of tuberculosis. The Edwards family took in Brainerd, their daughter Jerusha looked after him day and night, and his zeal for reaching the unreached got into their bones.

Unfortunately, first Brainerd and then shortly later Jerusha died, a tragic ending to what seemed to be a budding romance. Both deaths hit the family hard. This wasn't the first time that work with the Native Americans had become personal for the family, though. While Edwards was a boy, a relative of his had been captured in an Indian raid and had eventually married a native, taking up his lifestyle as well as his Catholic faith. If for no other reason, Edwards had been praying for Native Americans for years.

Because of the way he was moved by Brainerd's life and bravery, Edwards wrote a short biography about him, *The Life and Diary of David Brainerd*. Though Brainerd didn't witness any mass conversions, the story of his life went on to inspire men like William Carey, Robert Murray M'Cheyne, David Livingstone, Andrew Murray, and Jim Elliot, all of whom spoke of the importance of the biography for their lives and ministries. The book has never been out of print and has had an inestimable impact on global evangelization.

When the end of his pastorate had finally come, Edwards decided to take an offer to pastor a mission station among the Native Americans at Stockbridge, Massachusetts, where several family members had also worked. The project didn't see the fruits which Edwards had hoped for, but he had his hands full defending the small congregation of natives against many dishonest ploys of colonists.

Over time, the numbers of the station dwindled, partially because the English recruited the converts as soldiers, and partially because a group of the natives left to take part in the events that were adapted into the story *The Last of the Mohicans*. These setbacks notwithstanding, Edwards used the extra time at Stockbridge to write many of his most famous works, including the book you just read. In God's providence, the time was fruitful beyond what Edwards could have imagined.

University President

While Edwards was working in Stockbridge, one of his daughters courted and married the president of Princeton University. The university's spiritual outlook matched his own more than that of his alma mater, Yale, or of Harvard, so Edwards was probably excited about the match. Not long into the man's work, though, he died, and the board of directors at the college asked Edwards to consider stepping into the role to take over from his deceased son-in-law.

As I think about the development of Edwards's story line, this seems like a perfect, logical next step. It could have been the launching pad for whole movements of thought and scholarship, and he would almost certainly have thrived around so many other learned people. But unfortunately, only a month after taking his post, Edwards contracted smallpox from an inoculation meant to safeguard him against the illness, and he died not long thereafter. We can only speculate what consequences a ten- or twenty-year term at that post could have meant for him, for the college, and for evangelical Christianity.

Conclusion

As I said at the beginning of this short biographical sketch, the sheer number of jobs Edwards took upon himself amazes me. I can't help but compare him, in that respect, to Paul, who worked as a scholar, a preacher, a daredevil missionary, a resident scholar in Rome, a counselor to churches, and a prolific writer. This isn't to say that either man was perfect. I'm just beginning to read about Edwards's thoughts on slavery (the Edwards family owned a slave). And based on Edwards's study habits, I think it would be safe to call him a workaholic. But in all that, he sought to be a part of God's mission to expand His glory. In his dying words to his children, he made that point one last time, saying, "You are now to be left fatherless, which I hope will be an inducement to you all to seek a Father who will never fail you."

How I Adapted the Text

My only goal in this project was to make sure Edwards's ideas hit ordinary, non-academic people squarely between the eyes. I knew there were other resources available for understanding the man himself, examining the original text as closely as possible, and so on. So I just tried to remove any barrier between non-academics, who don't think of themselves as very theological, and this perspective-altering thesis. I feel like the thesis is a dagger through the heart of Christianity Lite, and I wanted to make the dagger as sharp as I could.

Some people might argue that Edwards's original wording and style make for a sharper dagger than mine. He definitely outdoes me in grammatical flair, but I think it's helpful to distinguish between first-rate thinking, which he certainly gave us in this book, and first-rate communication. The better you understand something, the less time it takes you to explain it. That's why we look at Jesus as both a first-rate thinker and a first-rate communicator. Jesus did not need complicated sentences and vocabulary to cut people to the heart. All that to say, I loved the ideas Edwards had to offer, but I don't think one has to use academic language to make deep, precise points.

My strategy evolved over the course of the project. While starting out, I made a draft that was easier to read but still very much a line-by-line paraphrase. I sent it to an Edwards scholar I knew, and he liked it but said that he "wondered if the text needs another pass, another revision, to make it even more concise and clear." At that point, the project began its slow morph from paraphrase to adaptation, and I'm very pleased with the title for that reason. I haven't simply paraphrased his book but have adapted it for modern readers, to meet their expectations for how a book should flow. Let me explain that process by talking about overall structural changes and then about a few updates and additions I made.

Overall Structure

First of all, Edwards originally structured the material into two "chapters" with different "sections." I made his two chapters into two "parts" and his different sections into individual "chapters." This seemed more natural, as few books of such length today have only two chapters.

His introduction to the book didn't tell us much about what to expect, so I added a short introduction which would help orient the modern reader for the journey. Also, because the first few pages of the book are (regrettably) the most complicated, many of my test readers got discouraged. Most of them asked me, "If this is the *introduction*, how impossible must the real meat of the book be?" For that reason, I thought it would be better to simply make his introduction "Chapter One."

Otherwise, I had two major concerns: to remove unnecessary repetitiveness, which even his most charitable fans say is a problem, and to make sure that the chapter endings made readers want to keep going. His introduction (now chapter 1), for example, originally ended without much of a bang. Add to that the fact that the material is very heady, and you understand why I quickly lost interest when I first tried to make it through this material in seminary.

To fix that particular problem, I took a paragraph from another chapter which seemed like it would make a good conclusion to chapter 1. Then I grafted it in to the natural flow of the material. The goal, of course, was simply to make sure that readers would *get* to chapter 2 in the first place. I did half a dozen little operations like that, and I feel like they went well enough that one doesn't notice the seams. Because I was drawing on his material, the chapters stay faithful to Edwards throughout.

Updates and Additions

Let me take a minute to talk about some particular situations where I either updated an analogy or added one. I had the same rationale in these individual cases as I did in the case of structural adjustments, but people who know and love Edwards's original text may be especially interested to hear about these emendations. Let me briefly walk through the chapters. Part 1 had many more of these changes than part 2.

First of all, the chapter titles themselves are mine. He gave the chapters titles such as, "Wherein It Is Considered How, on the Supposition of God's Making the Forementioned Things His Last End, He Manifests a Supreme and Ultimate Regard to Himself in All His Works." I found those a bit wordy and came up with shorter equivalents.

In part 1, chapter 1, I came up with new terms to explain his distinctions. He used "chief" and "ultimate," and I reworded them "highest" and "pure" so that they didn't sound so similar. The goal, after all, was to highlight a difference. I also updated several of his analogies, for example by switching an anecdote about a farmer to an anecdote about an entrepreneur. In another case, I substituted "jumping into a swimming pool for fun" for the idea of "eating a spoon full of honey on a whim."

Part 1, chapter 2, probably contains more additions and updates than any other section. I began here to rely on the classical trio of the "good, true, and beautiful" to encapsulate some of Edwards's ideas. I also added the first three paragraphs under the subhead "Value." Since this was the most crucial part of explaining his argument from logic, I spent a lot of time talking over the ideas with friends. For comprehension's sake, I added in a few of the ideas and rhetorical questions which had helped my friends most. Finally, I added the metaphor about love for painters logically exceeding love for their paintings.

In part 1, chapter 3, Edwards starts by speculating about whether God would have ever had a use for some of His attributes if He hadn't created the world. Michael Reeves helpfully calls this "unguarded language." Scholars can debate whether Edwards means what he seems to mean, but my interest was just to make sure that his otherwise brilliant point didn't get lost in the debate, so I streamlined the explanation. Finally, I tried to add some similar caveats when talking about whether there was an "inferior state of affairs" before we were here, and borrowed some C. S. Lewis–inspired language about praising our spouses and favorite institutions, as that relates to praising God.

In part 1, chapter 4, I thought a short discussion about pantheism, deism, and Christian theism would set up the material well, to avoid misunderstandings. I also added a definition of joy, as "a kind of desirable unrest and excitement about how good things are." Finally, I embellished a brief reference Edwards made to jewels. I thought that the metaphor of a jewel, or diamond, answered a major question that people have about the relationship of God's joy and ours, and I tried to flesh out the point along the lines which he himself hinted at briefly.

In part 1, chapter 5, I tried to bring some of his ideas to life in the fourth objection by using a reference to cheering for a sports team. The analogy was entirely mine, but I believe the underlying logic was his.

I can talk about part 2 much more quickly. I combined his first two chapters into a general introduction and then reformatted and edited down the second part of that introduction to build it around questions, which we later used in searching Scripture. I moved his chapter on glory closer to the front so that readers would understand that word before hitting the heaviest sections of Scripture that talk about it. I also used a bit of Speech Act Theory to illustrate what Edwards explained in that chapter. In chapters 3 and 4, I edited down some of his use of Scripture (if you can believe that) and tried to align the chapters' content structure with the questions I had raised in chapter 1, the introduction. Finally, I took the best components of his original conclusion and grafted them onto the end of chapter 5. The final chapter in this version is, as I stated there, completely my own material.

Because I know some people will want to compare my version with the original, I have tacked on Edwards's original introduction as the last appendix. For any who dare to work through it, it will definitely be an adventure. I hope you enjoyed my version, and thanks again for reading.

Jonathan Edwards's Original Introduction

"Containing Explanations of Terms and General Positions"

To avoid all confusion in our inquiries and reasonings, concerning the end for which God created the world, a distinction should be observed between the *chief end* for which an agent or efficient exerts any act and performs any work, and the *ultimate* end. These two phrases are not always precisely of the same signification: And tho' the *chief* end be always an *ultimate* end, yet every *ultimate* end is not always a chief end.

A chief end is opposite to an inferior end: An ultimate end, is opposite to a subordinate end. A subordinate end is something that an agent seeks and aims at in what he does; but yet don't seek it, or regard it at all upon it's own account, but wholly on the account of a further end, or in order to some other thing, which it is considered as a means of. Thus when a man that goes a journey to obtain a medicine to cure him of some disease, and restore his health,--the obtaining that medicine is his subordinate end; because 'tis not an end that he seeks for itself, or values at all upon its own account; but wholly as a means of a further end, viz. his health: Separate the medicine from that further end, and it is esteemed good for nothing; nor is it at all desired.

AN ultimate end is that which the agent seeks in what he does, for it's own sake: That he has respect to, as what he loves, values and takes pleasure in on it's own account, and not merely as a means of a further end: As when a man loves the taste of some particular sort of fruit, and is at pains and cost to obtain it, for the sake of the pleasure of that taste, which he values upon it's own account, as he loves his own pleasure; and not merely for the sake of any other good, which he supposes his enjoying that pleasure will be the means of.

SOME ends are subordinate ends, not only as they are subordinated to an ultimate end; but also to another end that is itself but a subordinate end: Yea, there may be a succession or chain of many subordinate ends, one dependent on another,-- one sought for another: The first for the next; and that for the sake of the next to that,--and so on in a long series before you come to any thing, that the agent aims at and seeks for it's own sake:--As when a man sells a garment to get money—to buy tools—to till his land—to obtain a crop—to supply him with food—to gratify his appetite. And he seeks to gratify his appetite, on it's own account, as what is grateful in itself. Here the end of his selling his garment, is to get money; but getting money is only a subordinate end: 'Tis not only subordinate to the last end, his gratifying his appetite; but to a nearer end, viz. his buying husbandry tools: And his obtaining these, is only a subordinate end, being only for the sake of tilling land: And the tillage of land, is an end not sought on it's own account, but for the sake of the crop to be produced: And the crop produced, is not an ultimate end, or an end sought for itself, but only for the sake of making bread: And the having bread, is not sought on it's own account, but for the sake of gratifying the appetite.

HERE the gratifying the appetite, is called the ultimate end; because 'tis the last in the chain, where a man's aim and pursuit stops and rests, obtaining in that, the thing finally aimed at. So whenever a man comes to that in which his desire terminates and rests, it being something valued on it's own account, then he comes to an ultimate end, let the chain be longer or shorter; yea, if there be but one link or one step that he takes before he comes to this end. As when a man that loves honey puts it into his mouth, for the sake of the pleasure of the taste, without aiming at any thing further. So that an end which an agent has in view, may be both his immediate and his ultimate end; his next and his last end. That end which is sought for the sake of itself, and not for the sake of a further end, is an ultimate end; it is ultimate or last, as it has no other beyond it, for whose sake it is, it being for the sake of itself: So that here, the aim of the agent stops and rests (without going further) being come to the good which he esteems a recompense of it's pursuit for it's own value.

HERE it is to be noted, that a thing sought, may have the nature of an ultimate, and also of a subordinate end, as it may be sought partly on its own account, and partly for the sake of a further end. Thus a man in what he does, may seek the love and respect of a particular person, partly on it's own account, because 'tis in itself agreable to men to be the objects of other's esteem and love: And partly, because he hopes, through the friendship of that person to have his assistance in other affairs; and so to be put under advantage for the obtaining further ends.

A chief end or highest end, which is opposite not properly to a subordinate end, but to an inferior end, is something diverse from an ultimate end. The chief end is an end that is most valued; and therefore most sought after by the agent in what he does. 'Tis evident, that to be an end more valued than another end, is not exactly the same thing as to be an end valued ultimately, or for it's own sake. This will appear, if it be considered.

1. THAT two different ends may be both ultimate ends, and yet not be chief ends. They may be both valued for their own sake, and both sought in the same work or acts, and yet one valued more highly and sought more than another: Thus a man may go a journey to obtain two different benefits or enjoyments, both which may be agreeable to him in themselves considered, and so both may be what he values on their own account and seeks for their own sake; And yet one may be much more agreable than the other: And so be what he sets his heart chiefly upon, and seeks most after in his going a journey. Thus a man may go a journey partly to obtain the possession and enjoyment of a bride that is very dear to him, and partly to gratify his curiosity in looking in a telescope, or some new-invented and extraordinary optic glass: Both may be ends he seeks in his journey, and the one not properly subordinate or in order to another. One may not depend on another; and therefore both may be ultimate ends: But yet the obtaining his beloved bride may be his chief end, and the benefit of the optic glass, his inferior end. The former may be what he sets his heart vastly most upon; and so be properly the chief end of his journey.

2. AN ultimate end is not always the chief end, because some subordinate ends may be more valued and sought after than some ultimate ends. Thus for instance, a man may aim at these two things in his going a journey; one may be to visit his friends, and another to receive a great estate, or a large sum of money that lies ready for him, at the place to which he is going. The latter, viz. his receiving the sum of money may be

but a subordinate end: He may not value the silver and gold on their own account, but only for the pleasure, gratifications and honor; that is the ultimate end, and not the money which is valued only as a means of the other. But yet the obtaining the money, may be what is more valued, and so an higher end of his journey, than the pleasure of seeing his friends; tho' the latter is what is valued on its own account, and so is an ultimate end.

BUT here several things may be noted:

FIRST, that when it is said that some subordinate ends may be more valued than some ultimate ends, 'tis not supposed that ever a subordinate end is more valued than that ultimate end or ends to which it is subordinate; because a subordinate end has no value, but what it derives from its ultimate end: For that reason it is called a subordinate end, because it is valued and sought, not for it's own sake, or it's own value, but only in subordination to a further end, or for the sake of the ultimate end, that it is in order to. But yet a subordinate end may be valued more than some other ultimate end that it is not subordinate to, but is independent of it, and don't belong to that series, or chain of ends. Thus for instance: If a man goes a journey to receive a sum of money, not at all as an ultimate end, or because he has any value for the silver and gold for their own sake, but only for the value of the pleasure and honor that the money may be a means of. In this case it is impossible that the subordinate end, viz. his having the money should be more valued by him than the pleasure and honor, for which he values it. It would be absurd to suppose that he values the means more than the end, when he has no value for the means but for the sake of the end, of which it is the means: But yet he may value the money, tho' but a subordinate end, more than some other ultimate end, to which it is not subordinate, and with which it has no connection. For instance, more than the comfort of a friendly visit; which was one end of his journey.

SECONDLY, Not only is a subordinate end never superior to that ultimate end, to which it is subordinate; but the ultimate end is always (not only equal but) superior to it's subordinate end, and more valued by the agent; unless it be when the ultimate end entirely depends on the subordinate: So that he has no other means by which to obtain his last end, and also is looked upon as certainly connected with it,—then the subordinate end may be as much valued as the last end; because the last end, in such a case, does altogether depend upon, and is wholly and certainly conveyed by it. As for instance, if a pregnant woman has a peculiar appetite to a certain rare fruit that is to be found only in the garden of a particular friend of her's, at a distance; and she goes a journey to go to her friend's house or garden, to obtain that fruit--the ultimate end of her journey, is to gratify that strong appetite; The obtaining that fruit, is the subordinate end of it. If she looks upon it, that the appetite can be gratified by no other means than the obtaining that fruit; and that it will certainly be gratified if she obtains it, then she will value the fruit as much as she values the gratification of her appetite. But otherwise, it will not be so: If she be doubtful whether that fruit will satisfy her craving, then she will not value it equally with the gratification of her appetite itself; or if there be some other fruit that she knows of, that will gratify her desire, at least in part; which she can obtain without such inconvenience or trouble as shall countervail the gratification; which is in effect, frustrating her of her last end, because her last end is the pleasure of gratifying her appetite, without any trouble that shall countervail, and in effect destroy it. Or if it be so, that her appetite cannot be gratified without this fruit, nor yet with it alone, without something else to be compounded with it,—then her value for her last end will be divided between these several ingredients as so many subordinate, and no one alone will be equally valued with the last end.

HENCE it rarely happens among mankind, that a subordinate end is equally valued with it's last end; because the obtaining of a last end rarely depends on one single, uncompounded means, and is infallibly connected with that means: Therefore, mens last ends are commonly their highest ends.

THIRDLY, If any being has but one ultimate end, in all that he does, and there be a great variety of operations, his last end may justly be looked upon as his *supreme* end: For in such a case, every other end but that one, is an end to that end; and therefore no other end can be superior to it. Because, as was observed before, a subordinate end is never more valued, than the end to which it is subordinate.

MOREOVER, the subordinate effects, events or things brought to pass, which all are means of this end, all uniting to contribute their share towards the obtaining the one last end, are very various; and therefore, by what has been now observed, the ultimate end of all must be valued, more than any one of the particular means. This seems to be the case with the works of God, as may more fully appear in the sequel.

FROM what has been said, to explain what is intended by an ultimate end, the following things may be observed concerning ultimate ends in the sense explained.

FOURTHLY, Whatsoever any agent has in view in any thing he does, which he loves, or which is an immediate gratification of any appetite or inclination of nature; and is agreable to him in itself, and not merely for the sake of something else, is regarded by that agent as his last end. The same may be said, of avoiding of that which is in itself painful or disagreable: For the avoiding of what is disagreable is agreable. This will be evident to any bearing in mind the meaning of the terms. By last end being meant, that which is regarded and sought by an agent, as agreable or desirable for it's own sake; a subordinate that which is sought only for the sake of something else.

FIFTHLY, From hence it will follow, that, if an agent in his works has in view more things than one that will be brought to pass by what he does, that are agreable to him, consider'd in themselves, or what he loves and delights in on their own account,—then he must have more things than one that he regards as his last ends in what he does. But if there be but one thing that an agent seeks, as the consequence of what he does that is agreable to him, on it's own account, then there can be but one last end which he has in all his actions and operations.

BUT only here a distinction must be observed of things which may be said to be agreable to an agent, in themselves consider'd in two senses. (1.) What is in itself grateful to an agent, and valued and loved on its own account, *simply* and *absolutely* considered, and is so universally and originally, antecedent to and *independent* of all conditions, or any supposition of particular cases and circumstances. And (2.) What may be said to be in itself agreable to an agent, *hypothetically* and consequentially: Or, on supposition or condition of such and such circumstances or on the happening of such a particular case. Thus, for instance: A man may originally love society. An inclination to society may be implanted in his very nature: And society may be agreable to him antecedent to all presupposed cases and circumstances: And this may cause him to seek a family. And the comfort of society may be originally his last end, in seeking a family. But after he has a family, peace, good order and mutual justice and friendship in his family, may be agreable to him, and what he delights in for their own sake: and therefore these things may be his last end in many things he does in the government and regulation of his family. But they were not his original end with respect to his family. The justice and peace of a family was not properly his last end before he had a family, that induced him to seek a family, but consequentially. And the case being put of his having a family, then these things wherein the good order and beauty of a family consist, become his last end in many things he does in such circumstances. In like manner we must suppose that God before he created the world, had some good in view, as a consequence of the world's existence that was originally agreable to him in itself considered, that inclined him to create the world, or bring the universe, with various intelligent creatures into existence in such a manner as he created it. But after the world was created, and such and such intelligent creatures actually had existence, in such and such circumstances, then a wise, just regulation of them was agreable to God, in itself considered. And God's love of justice, and hatred of injustice, would be sufficient in such a case to induce God to deal justly with his creatures, and to prevent all injustice in him towards them. But yet there is no necessity of supposing, that God's love of doing justly to intelligent beings, and hatred of the contrary, was what originally induced God to create the world, and make intelligent beings; and so to order the occasion of doing either justly or unjustly. The justice of God's nature makes a just regulation agreable, and the contrary disagreable, as there is occasion, the subject being supposed, and the occasion given: But we must suppose something else that should incline him to create the subjects or order the occasion.

So that perfection of God which we call his faithfulness,

or his inclination to fulfil his promises to his creatures, could not properly be what moved him to create the world; nor could such a fulfillment of his promises to his creatures, be his last end, in giving the creatures being. But yet after the world is created, after intelligent creatures are made, and God has bound himself by promise to them, then that disposition which is called his faithfulness may move him in his providential disposals towards them: And this may be the end of many of God's works of providence, even the exercise of his faithfulness in fulfilling his promises. And may be in the lower sense his last end. Because faithfulness and truth must be supposed to be what is in itself amiable to God, and what he delights in for its own sake. Thus God may have ends of particular works of providence, which are ultimate ends in a lower sense, which were not ultimate ends of the creation.

So that here we have two sorts of ultimate ends; one of which may be called an *original,* and independent ultimate end; the other *consequential* and dependent. For 'tis evident, the latter sort are truly of the nature of ultimate ends: Because, tho' their being agreable to the agent, or the agent's desire of them, be consequential on the existence, or supposition of proper subjects and occasion; yet the subject and occasion being supposed, they are agreable and amiable in themselves. We may suppose that to a righteous Being, the doing justice between two parties, with whom he is concerned, is agreable in itself, and is loved for it's own sake, and not merely for the sake of some other end: And yet we may suppose, that a desire of doing justice between two parties, may be consequential on the being of those parties, and the occasion given.

THEREFORE I make a distinction between an end that in this manner is *consequential,* and a *subordinate* end.

IT may be observed, that when I speak of God's ultimate end in the creation of the world, in the following discourse, I commonly mean in that highest sense, viz. the original ultimate end.

SIXTHLY, It may be further observed, that the original ultimate end or ends of the creation of the world is *alone,* that which induces God to give the occasion for consequential ends, by the first creation of the world, and the original disposal of it. And the more original the end is, the more extensive and universal it is. That which God had primarily in view in creating, and the original ordination of the world, must be constantly kept in view, and have a governing influence in all God's works, or with respect to every thing that he does towards his creatures.

AND therefore,

SEVENTHLY, If we use the phrase ultimate end in this highest sense, then the same that is God's ultimate end in creating the world, if we suppose but one such end, must be what he makes his ultimate aim in all his works, in every thing he does either in creation or providence. But we must suppose that in the use which God puts the creatures to that he hath made, he must evermore have a regard to the end, for which he has made them. But if we take *ultimate end* in the other lower sense, God may sometimes have regard to those things as ultimate ends, in particular works of providence, which could not in any proper sense be his last end in creating the world.

EIGHTHLY, On the other hand, whatever appears to be God's ultimate end in any sense, of his works of providence in general, that must be the ultimate end of the work of creation itself. For tho' it be so that God may act for an end, that is an ultimate end in a lower sense, in some of his works of providence, which is not the ultimate end of the creation of the world: Yet this doth not take place with regard to the works of providence in general. But we may justly look upon whatsoever has the nature of an ultimate end of God's works of providence in general, that the same is also an ultimate end of the creation of the world; for God's works of providence in general, are the same with the general use that he puts the world to that he has made. And we may well argue from what we see of the general use which God makes of the world, to the general end for which he designed the world. Tho' there may be some things that are ends of particular works of providence, that were not the last end of the creation, which are in themselves grateful to God in such particular emergent circumstances; and so are last ends in an inferior sense: Yet this is only in certain cases, or particular occasions. But if they are last ends of God's proceedings in the use of the world in general, this shews that his making them last ends don't depend on particular cases and circumstances, but the nature of things in general, and his general design in the being and constitution of the universe.

NINETHLY, If there be but one thing that is originally, and independent on any future, supposed cases, agreable to God, to be obtained by the creation of the world, then there can be but one last end of God's work, in this highest sense. But if there are various things, properly diverse one from another, that are, absolutely and independently on the supposition of any future given cases, agreable to the divine being, which are actually obtained by the creation of the world, then there were several ultimate ends of the creation, in that highest sense.

ABOUT THE AUTHOR

Ben Stevens (MDiv, Trinity Evangelical Divinity School) lives in Berlin, Germany, with his wife, Becky. He has written for *The Washington Times, The Huffington Post, First Things, Christianity Today, Relevant,* and *The Gospel Coalition Blog.* Keep up with him at twitter.com/benwstevens.